MW01278074

WTF?
WHERE'S THE
FRAUD?

*How to Unmask and Stop Identity
Fraud's Drain on Our Government*

Larry Benson and Andy Bucholz

<ARCHWAY
PUBLISHING>

Archway Publishing books may be ordered through booksellers or by contacting:

Archway Publishing
1663 Liberty Drive
Bloomington, IN 47403
www.archwaypublishing.com
1 (888) 242-5904

Because of the dynamic nature of the Internet, any web addresses or
links contained in this book may have changed since publication and
may no longer be valid. The views expressed in this work are solely those
of the author and do not necessarily reflect the views of the publisher,
and the publisher hereby disclaims any responsibility for them.

Any people depicted in stock imagery provided by Thinkstock are models,
and such images are being used for illustrative purposes only.
Certain stock imagery © Thinkstock.

ISBN: 978-1-4808-2560-4 (sc)
ISBN: 978-1-4808-2561-1 (hc)
ISBN: 978-1-4808-2562-8 (e)

Library of Congress Control Number: 2015920795

Print information available on the last page.

Archway Publishing rev. date: 12/22/2015

CONTENTS

LIST OF COMMONLY USED ACRONYMS

DHS	Department of Homeland Security
DMV	Department of Motor Vehicles
DMF	Death Master File
FTC	Federal Trade Commission
GAO	Government Accountability Office
HHS	Department of Health and Human Services
IRS	Internal Revenue Service
PII	Personal Identifying Information
RMV	Registry of Motor Vehicles
SSA	Social Security Administration
SSN	Social Security number

FOREWORD

Lying, like dancing, takes two. Both rely on a strong leader, and a partner willing to follow. When lying, you must be both confident and determined. You have to steer the lie the exact way you need it to go, otherwise you could end up knocking over the punch bowl in the corner. Your dance partner must be able to follow the lie, and believe it.

I am no dance expert, but I am an expert at deception. For several years, telling quick lies and impersonating other people was my livelihood. I was effective, though unwise. Before I was 22 years old, I convinced people I was a doctor, a lawyer, a security guard, a professor, and even a pilot. At that time, the crucial part of the act was not mine, but my partner's. For the lie to be successful, my partner had to believe the lie I was putting before their eyes.

Today, this particular kind of lying, identity theft, has changed. It is far simpler than it used to be: There is no couple dancing around each other. Today, you don't have to rent a costume and walk with confidence. Today, there is no one you have to convince. The government agencies will dance with anyone, freely giving benefits, often more than once, to just about anyone who asks.

Today's identity fraud allows for the convenience of sitting at home in your pajamas plugging numbers into a computer. Many government agencies rely on self-reported data that allows fraudsters to perpetrate identity fraud in bulk. When I was pulling scams, I could only do one at a time. I needed my dance partner to believe the lie I was telling. Now, self-reported data takes away one of the biggest blockades to identity fraud: that of an agency's perception.

Self-reported data does not elicit doubts, as all the information these systems receive are perceived as true. Back in 2001, I authored a book called *The Art of the Steal*, where I noted that identity theft would be the crime of the future. Unfortunately, I was right. Over the last few years, we have watched identity theft explode into a booming criminal industry. In 2007, I published another book entirely dedicated to preventing identity theft.

Despite our best efforts, however, identity theft has only grown. Now, it is more prevalent than ever. Currently, there is a victim in the United States every two seconds. Identity theft is one of the most insidious crimes because it can truly wreck someone's life. Unlike more violent crimes or physical robberies, identity theft steals *you*: your past, and your future. Identity theft allows criminals to cripple individuals, from college graduates trying to start their life with a first credit card to elderly people in nursing homes whose life savings suddenly evaporate. Identity theft acts as a doorway through which people have unlimited potential: with someone else's identity, the options are almost limitless. Have money in the bank? It can disappear. Have good credit? It can dry up in minutes. If I can become you, what I can do is only limited by my imagination—buy a car in your name, get a mortgage in your name, obtain a job in your name, receive benefits in your name, and even commit a crime in your name.

Back when I was assuming different identities, I never took on the guise of one specific individual. My goal was always to portray myself as a type of person by taking on a specific occupation. Now, identity theft has become more targeted. When you steal a person's identity, you take on their most personal aspects. You have to become that person in a myriad of ways, but most specifically through their Social Security number. When I was working on the other side of the law, I was most focused on using fraudulent checks to fund my adventures. Check fraud required a lot of work: the right tools such as a printing press, the correct paper and ink, an operating knowledge of the checks and banks you're looking to defraud, and a winning personality to help smooth out any kinks in your performance. Technology certainly helped make check fraud more feasible by making high quality printers and embossing tools available to the public. Scanners and color copiers are a fraudster's dream. Today it is still technology that is moving the fraud game forward. Now, though, the technology is almost entirely online, in code and programming, nonphysical tools that, in the wrong hands, can be used to amass huge amounts of money and wreck lives.

Even though the technology fraudsters use has changed, some of the same rules seem to apply. Whether someone is using a fake ATM machine simply to scan credit and debit cards (yes, this is an actual scam that people have pulled), or taking advantage of a long-term identity theft, such as stealing the identity of an infant and taking advantage of it for the next eighteen years, simplicity is always the key. The criminal mind works as if it's always solving some sort of puzzle, and finding the easiest and quickest solution is the way to sort it out. Stealing someone's identity requires almost daily attention. Being a fraudster is like having a full-time job (which is why I advise employers to be wary of employees who never take advantage of their vacation time, as they may be working for themselves on the side).

Streamlining these schemes is essential, especially since the current technology allows for so many different schemes to go on at once. Identity thefts are not usually elaborate criminal exploits, but are more likely to be connected with an administrator or employee pocketing a few forms and filling out tax returns with the stolen information on it. These schemes can be as simple as changing the address to a P.O. box from which you can collect the money. What I want to emphasize is that identity theft is easy. It's easy to pull off, it's easy to reconcile with yourself from a moral standpoint (much more so than mugging someone at knifepoint), and it's easy not to get caught. What isn't as easy, it seems, is stopping it.

Prevention of identity theft has come a long way since 2007, but we still have a long way to go. When there is a system in place, there is always someone out there who can defeat it, or who already has. Our world will always have criminals who are looking to beat the system, or to work around it. What we need to do is stay ahead of them, instead of having them stay ahead of us. By having technology work for us instead of the fraudsters, we have a chance of staying ahead of the criminal mind.

Identity theft and identity frauds are increasing every day. Crooks are finding new and inventive ways to bilk the system. Unfortunately, not everyone is taking this problem as seriously as they should. Government agencies often don't realize the kind of strain fraud-related crimes put on our economy, and the more dangerous threats that fraud also poses. In my years of advising agencies on identity fraud, forgery, embezzlement, secure documents, and identity theft, I've seen million dollar losses turn into billion dollar losses. What we have not seen -- *until now* -- is the world of mass data breaches, where one hacker, with a single keystroke, can take down entire business customer files and government databases. The last three years have seen several companies that are household names lose credibility and customer trust. Our data is out there, and we are not taking the adequate steps to keep it secure. The book you are about to read tells a cautionary tale about the latest wave of fraud, this wave against our government, and why it is so dangerous. Unless we take proactive steps to cut down on fraud, it will only get worse. Take it from me, catching a fraudster is not as easy as it looks. Education is the key, and this book will help.

Frank W. Abagnale

Frank Abagnale
Subject of the book, movie and Broadway musical, "Catch Me If You Can".

INTRODUCTION

Government fraud tied to identity theft is the largest, fastest growing crime in America. Yet, most people don't recognize the danger it poses to millions of Americans and our economy.

Remember that old story where Jacob literally pulls the wool over his father Isaac's eyes? He uses a goat's skin to fool his father into thinking that Jacob is his older brother Esau, in order to win a blessing from Isaac. Identity theft has always been with us, even from the time of the Old Testament.

Today, technology has opened the door to identity theft on an unprecedented scale. Millions of people are probably already affected, some seriously, and many without even realizing that their identities have been stolen.

Consider the story of Carter Andrushko. He was five years old when his mother applied for Medicaid -- and discovered that someone had been using his Social Security number. The assistant attorney general in Utah, where the family lives, told Jennifer Andrushko that thousands of Social Security numbers are sold on the streets daily. A large-scale study by Carnegie Mellon University done in 2009-2010 found that more than 10% of the 76 million children, 7.6 million kids, have likely been victims of identity theft. That's a staggering number. If Carter and those other kids are lucky, they won't have a problem later in life when they go to apply for their first job or credit card, or when they want to buy a house. But there's no way to know. Once your identity is stolen, it can't be returned.

You might be saying: This is old news. I've heard about banks and big stores coping with identity theft for years. But what's new now, and the reason we're writing this book, is how stolen identities are being used: to steal from the government in ways that affect all of us.

Identity theft for government benefits and payments is growing at an unprecedented rate. Two decades ago, you applied for government benefits, like Social Security or your driver's license, with paper and often in person. Stealing someone's identity using those old-fashioned systems was arduous: Thieves had to steal identities one person at a time, and there was a good chance they would be spotted. In-person human judgment and intuition on the part of the people behind the desks in the brick-and-mortar buildings kept many frauds from occurring.

Today, many government agencies have done away with in-person applications (one exception, thankfully, is getting your first drivers license, which has to be done in person). Online application systems for government benefits have created a backdoor through which fraudsters can rip off the government. It's easy for a 15-year-old criminal to file for Social Security benefits online, using a stolen number that belongs to a 65-year-old woman: No one ever sees him, and there's nothing built into the system to check to make sure that a filer is who he or she claims to be. Anonymous payments, specifically on pre-paid debit cards, have made it even easier to perpetrate this kind of fraud. Again, no one ever sees that the recipient of the card isn't who he ought to be.

Really? We hear you asking. Why didn't the government build safeguards in? There are literally billions of dollars, trillions of dollars at stake. That's what we ask ourselves.

HOW DID THIS HAPPEN?

Two technological advancements and a huge breakdown in government oversight allow fraudsters to break the law while remaining virtually anonymous. Since the Internet became a part of daily life, government agencies decided to take advantage of the ease and convenience the Internet offered. Those agencies began to interact with taxpayers online. That was the first advancement. Second, agencies started paying out benefits online, and through pre-paid debit cards. All of a sudden, people could apply for their government benefits online. The Internet became a ubiquitous force, but with little regulation. So, when did the breakdown in oversight happen? Believe it or not – we will offer plenty of examples as the book goes on – government agencies often do not even bother to make the most basic checks of people who are applying for benefits. For instance, a fraudster can tell a state's department of revenue (DOR) she made $3 million and deserves a $2.1 million refund, and the DOR will send it to her! No questions asked.

In a way, the Internet is working as a veil, where the American government sends benefits anonymously to recipients whose faces they've never even seen. What used to be a white-collar crime, with one person ripping off another individual's identity, has been transformed into a crime that can be perpetrated by low-level criminals, and that can occur en masse, in just a few hours time.

Government fraud is turning into a multi-billion dollar industry, with little-to-no solid numbers on just how much is going on. Because fraud is so underreported, we can't even imagine the full dollar amounts that are being stolen, though this book pulls together the data that exists on the topic.

In 2014, 47% of American adults had their information exposed by hackers, with the total number of hacked accounts in the range of 432 million.[1] With the number of Americans only at 315 million as of late 2014, that means that not only do Americans have multiple accounts to be hacked, but that these same accounts have been exposed multiple times.

The bottom line here is that people no longer have to walk up to a counter where identification is requested and verified in person. Our government agencies are moving these processes online,

---

[1] Pagliery, "Half of American Adults Hacked This Year," 2014

meaning they are not verifying whom they're interacting with, and it's costing all of us.

These schemes are so lucrative that criminals can't keep up with the money. In fact, identity theft gets drug dealers off the streets because the risk of being caught at this kind of crime is almost zero, and the profit unlimited. Criminals are hosting "Rain Parties" where classes on how to steal identities and file for refunds in mass quantities are taught. As payment, kickbacks are given to the instructor for every refund obtained from either the Internal Revenue Service (IRS) or State Departments of Revenue. One of the biggest problems with identity fraud, aside from being highly lucrative, is that the chances of arrest and prosecution are incredibly low.

If it looks like a book club, it's probably a book club. That is, unless it's a symposium on how to steal billions of dollars. With the broad use of the Internet, the ease of access to data and information, and the technical prowess of the next generation, this problem becomes even more pervasive. Technology is making a huge leap forward in fraudulent practices. What is the long-term impact? How much is it costing me? My government? Quick answers: huge, a lot, and even more.

We wrote this book as an alarm to policymakers and agency heads who should pay attention to the risk, measure how widespread it is, and take steps to stop it. In this book, we're going to explain what we see is happening, illustrate the holes in the system that allow criminals access, and outline a multi-tiered plan to make our data more secure.

Every person has a responsibility to protect his or her own identity, too. Every day we give our personal information out, putting our identities at risk, and every day, criminals are stealing that personal information. Maybe yours. Maybe today. Identity fraud is not some pop-eyed concoction of would-be criminals, it's real, and it's right under our noses. It's in our dentists' offices and children's schools, it's in our email accounts and trash bins. It's everywhere, and it's getting worse.

Many people insist that this doesn't happen to them. They insist they don't just leave their personal information lying around. But people leave themselves vulnerable in ways they're not even aware of. Who is this dumb? We all are, you, me, helpless taxpayers and people who are just living their lives and following the rules. Think, did your last doctor's office form ask for your Social Security number? If so, did you list it on the form? Did your son or daughter signing up for classes at university unwittingly hand over Social Security number, all former addresses and emails to the Registrar's office that doesn't have a clue about how to keep them safe? How about when you signed up to volunteer at the local tutoring organization, that does a quick background check? In addition to making some recommendations about how government and policymakers should reform the system, we will make some suggestions about how you can and should take steps and make it a habit to protect your data.

So how extensive is this problem really, what programs are being defrauded, and how can we stop this from happening? The first step is simply admitting that the problem exists. Most agencies agree that fraud exists within their programs, but most agencies claim the fraud rate in their program is *one percent or less*. Many agencies hide from scrutiny by claiming that fraud is a very low and controlled percentage of any given program. Various officials we have met with make this claim. But in private, most officials will admit to having no idea what the true percentage is. One state unemployment commissioner told us, "We have no idea how bad the fraud rate is. We hope it is less than 15 percent." Until agencies admit that identity fraud is taking a much larger chunk out of their funds, adequate budgeting to truly solve the problem will never take place. So to answer your incredibly reasonable question: fraud is extremely prolific, and even more so than we know.

WHO ARE WE, TO BE TALKING ABOUT FRAUD?

Our interest in and knowledge about identity fraud started almost by accident. We are Larry Benson and Andy Bucholz, a director and vice president at LexisNexis. Helping the government manage data is our work. But in the course of doing our jobs, we realized governments -- local, state and national -- aren't doing much of anything to protect us from fraud.

It started like this: Larry started clipping articles to send to his team of salespeople, responsible for selling LexisNexis services to governments, so they would understand what governments were up against.

Larry's team started forwarding theses articles to their contacts in government, and before you know it, *Fraud of the Day*, our daily email newsletter, was born. After national conferences and lectures, 17,000 subscribers and one website later, Fraud of the Day has gone from a funny email chain to a widely read publication on government fraud. Over 1,000 articles have been written covering 40 different topics to date. With Andy being a highly regarded fraud expert and frequent speaker, an ex-cop, and self-proclaimed data-geek, we are trying to make government fraud a national priority, and shed some light on just how big of a deal it is.

We are just two managers who take serious advantage of Casual Friday, but we've developed a passion for this issue. We take it seriously, and so should you.

Later on in the book, we'll talk about how identity theft and government fraud have enabled some of the worst crimes in history. The 19 terrorists who perpetrated 9/11 attacks had 30 drivers' licenses between them, from Virginia, Florida, Maryland, Arizona and California. Those fake drivers licenses enabled them to avoid the terrorist watch lists.

Guess what? Not much has changed since then. New terrorists acting today could take the same steps, get more fake drivers licenses, and use them in new ways to attack us.

If you're afraid that we're telling the criminals how to do this, don't worry. The criminals already know. We're telling you, because you most likely don't.

Now that you've been standing in the bookstore for 10 minutes, thumbing through the introduction and trying to make sense of this book, what's your next step? This is not just about your own money. This is about how your tax dollars are being preserved and spent where they should be. This is about keeping your children's identities safe so you and they can sleep at night. It's about your information being your own, and nobody else's. It's about keeping our country safe. There's no reason to wait around until you or your family members become the next headline about identity fraud. It's time to get informed. It's time to stop allowing criminals to turn us all into victims. It's time to turn the page.

CHAPTER ONE

Identity Theft: Why You Should Care And How Much It Costs Us

It's early September, and yet the Tampa air is hot and heavy. The summer makes everybody sluggish. Even the drug dealers have been taking a summer-long siesta, or so it appeared at first to the local police forces. In 2012, drug-related crimes dropped.

Then, that same fall, a Tampa Postal Inspector found IRS debit cards that were destined for criminals in the Tampa area, and valued at over $100 million dollars. It turns out that drug dealers and other criminals were no longer content with silly pocket change. In the past several years, known dealers have been found with laptops, lists of names, Social Security numbers, addresses, and hundreds of preloaded debit cards from the IRS. The influx of debit cards is so great that the criminals don't even have the time to cash them. Law enforcement believes that this is a one billion dollar annual crime in *just the Tampa area alone.*

This is only one of thousands of fraud stories you can find in the news if you look. There are massive data breaches. There are people who have been able to steal millions from the government. And there are people who did nothing wrong, whose lives are filled with worry and concern and more hardship than they deserve because of identity theft. The elderly are disproportionately victims of identity fraud.

Take the case of Willie Chaney, a 74-year-old man living on Social Security in Atlanta. One day, the bank called to tell him he didn't have enough money to cover a withdrawal. Did he lose track of the balance?

Nope. His Social Security check had been docked to pay off a student loan that had been taken out in his name, so that this 74-year-old retired truck driver in Atlanta could go to Rio Salado Community College in Tempe Arizona. Mr. Chaney told a local TV news reporter he couldn't even pick out Arizona on a map. Meanwhile, the U.S. Department of Education turned down his request to discharge the loan because the government sent him the wrong form.[2]

These stories will only grow more common unless the government acts now safeguarding our identities, and detecting and stopping fraud. We know you're smart (you decided to read this book, so obviously you're a genius), but we'll start with the basics. What is identity fraud?

WHAT IS IDENTITY FRAUD?

Identity theft is a stepping-stone to enable identity fraud, in which an individual pretends to be someone else by taking on that person's identity, usually as a method to gain access to resources or obtain credit and other benefits in that person's name. Especially in our new, technological age, identity theft is a fairly hands-off process: there's no acting (well, except for that one guy who pretended to be his mom, but we'll get to that later), kidnapping, or plastic surgery necessary. All someone needs are some key ingredients to create a

---

[2] Fowle, "Department of Education threatens to dock man's social security check," 2015, http://www.fox5atlanta.com/news/2598897-story (accessed Oct. 13, 2015).

convincing portrait of another person, usually their name, address, Social Security number, and date of birth. With these simple pieces of information, a fraudster can pass themselves off as almost anyone, especially when no one is looking. The modern forms of identity theft and identity fraud began to show up in the headlines about 15 years ago. You might remember this: Thieves rifled through mail, swiping pieces of paper that allowed them to apply for credit cards in your name. (In reality, this happens much less than we think, but the idea somehow stuck in the public consciousness). Some thieves got more sophisticated: They stole credit card numbers from receipts at restaurants or stores. Or, in some audacious cases, as Frank wrote in the introduction, thieves set up fake ATMs that were used to steal thousands of ATM card numbers and passwords. Presto! Your bank account could be emptied.

In response, financial institutions and other big companies stepped up their game. Lawmakers forced them to take financial responsibility for fraud, and as a result, many of them now have systems that require you to have multiple passwords and to submit to short quizzes before you gain access to your accounts. They're not foolproof, but they stop wholesale theft. This kind of identity fraud still happens, and it can be a real pain to replace your credit or ATMs cards.

However, the damage resulting from the latest wave of fraud is much greater. We're talking about fraud that targets government agencies. This kind of fraud uses the same basic format we've seen before: Someone steals information that allows him or her to pose as another person. But instead of having the wherewithal to respond with tighter security systems, as the big companies did, government agencies are sitting ducks.

When it comes to identity fraud, it takes two: one to deceive, and one to believe. If someone in a bar approached you claiming to be an astronaut in a sad, and slightly desperate attempt to impress you, would you believe him or her? If you do, you have to assume some responsibility in your own poor decision-making. It takes one to deceive and one to believe.

Government agencies believe every single astronaut that walks into the bar. In the past decade, most government agencies have gotten rid of the application processes that required you to visit a brick-and-mortar building and interact with a human. A 25-year-old identity thief had a much harder time passing himself off as a 5-year-old girl when he had to do it in person.

When agencies move their interactions online, they start to rely exclusively on self-reported data, supposedly true information given to them over the Internet, provided by an individual. Whether that individual looks like, sounds like, or even is the right age to be an "astronaut" does not even come into the equation. The information being reported by individuals is taken as true, and in many instances, is not actually verified *at all*.

It's like having a 13-year-old child who starts using the Internet. Do we innately trust that the person she's talking to on the other end is actually her friend Sonia from gym class, or do we have an ever-present fear that Sonia is actually a 40-year old axe murderer? If you're like most parents you do some verification. You give Sonia's parents a call, and you look over your kids' texts, too, not every single one, but enough to get a handle on what they're doing. All of these situations depend on the trust you have that the person interacting with you is actually who they say they are, that their self-reported data checks out. Unfortunately, when it comes to government benefits, the fake astronauts are convincing our agencies to stay and have another drink. Their information is compelling enough to slip through the cracks, and the verification checks on the other end that should be performed are not happening.

Here are a few examples of stories from the world of identity theft, which offer a sense of how porous the government's controls on our information are:

• In 2012, according to a story on the New York City TV channel PIX11, some Tufts University students attending the Macy's Thanksgiving Day parade took a close look at the confetti falling around them: The strips of paper contained personal information, including phone numbers and Social Security numbers. On closer inspection, the students discovered the confetti were records from Long Island's Nassau County police department. They'd been shredded, probably by the identity thieves – but not shredded enough. The confetti even contained names of undercover police officers.

• That same year, in Wisconsin, the state Department of Revenue acknowledged posting online by mistake the tax numbers of tens of thousands of businesses and consumers -- at least the fourth time in six years the state has released confidential information and raised the fear of identity fraud. The state planned to offer free credit monitoring to consumers affected by the mistaken release - at a cost of up to $600,000.[3]

When information falls into the hands of a fraudster, what happens? It is used as a tool for people to obtain government benefits with barely a second thought. How about this lead from the *Washington Free Beacon* in 2015: "The Social Security Administration (SSA) paid individuals acting as representatives for disabled beneficiaries nearly $50 million even though they were dead." An audit uncovered the payments, which were an average $1,182.24 a month.[4]

One woman was able to obtain 50 different identities— and by using self-reported data she concurrently received unemployment benefits from eight different states, ranging from Alaska to Pennsylvania to Utah. (We're not terrific at geography over here, but last time we checked, Alaska and Pennsylvania are pretty far apart!)

---

[3] Milwaukee Journal Sentinel. "State mistake puts thousands at risk of identity theft," July 24, 2012.
[4] Washington Free Beacon. "Social Security paid the dead $47M, says audit," June 25, 2015.

For most of the identities, she obtained personal information online. Even while she collected unemployment with all of these stolen identities, she was using her own name and identity to collect Social Security benefits. The woman used some of the identities to open bank accounts or cash cards over the Internet, and deposited the fraudulent benefits into those accounts tied to the stolen identities. Later, she withdrew the money from an automated teller machine. So why is it that this woman wasn't caught any number of times? By using self-reported data, she essentially became invisible, and was able to hide behind any one of the fifty identities she stole at any given time. The problem at the heart of this story, and of so many other identity fraud stories, is the same: There was no identity verification that double-checked this woman's activity.[5]

Most government agencies require only three or four key data-points of self-reported information to confirm identities and distribute funds or benefits: a name, Social Security number, date of birth and or the address. The data doesn't even have to perfectly align: A fraudster could have a Social Security number and make up a birthdate to go along -- and most agencies would never even realize. For government agencies, it makes a lot of sense to use the Internet as a way to give out benefits faster and more efficiently. Without the person-to-person contact, however, there is far less accurate verification happening.

WHO ARE THE FRAUDSTERS?

Mugging someone is a physical crime. It involves seeing the fear on victims' faces, watching their hands shake as they reach for their wallet, perhaps hearing pleas that they have children. An in-person robbery is a visceral experience, putting the criminal right there with their target. Identity fraud is much more damaging than stealing a

---

[5] Office of the Inspector General, 2013

wallet, but far more people are willing to do it, perhaps because it does not feel like stealing. People who would never steal a wallet might steal someone's identity. If someone told you that a house on your street had $100,000 cash sitting right inside, would you take it? What if that money was sitting in a burlap sack on the front yard, one hundred dollar bills blowing like errant leaves? Would you take it then?

The psychology of identity theft and identity fraud is complicated. Why some people give in to temptation and others don't is a question that experts far smarter than us have studied. But we do know that identity fraud is a crime of opportunity. Doctors, tax preparers, secretaries, workers at the DMV, all commit fraud. Insurance agents, postal workers – all have been caught committing identity fraud. It's too easy: Once people realize they can make a few extra bucks on the side, they get sucked right into it.

Take, for example, a Florida prison guard accused of stealing personal information from state corrections databases and using it to file 182 fraudulent income tax returns to get refunds. The guard stole the personal information for current and former inmates by cutting and pasting the info from Florida Department of Corrections databases into his own personal files (very high-tech fraud happening here!). The man allegedly used the information to file fraudulent tax returns seeking refunds of more than $500,000, and now faces up to 20 years in prison.[6]

The fraudsters come from all walks of life. Identity thieves are young and old, of every race and ethnicity, religion, and socio-economic class. There are homeless fraudsters and millionaire fraudsters, student fraudsters and bus driver fraudsters. In reality, a fraudster can be anyone.

When we ask a room full of people where they think identities are being stolen from the most—and who the most worrisome kind

---

[6] The Associated Press, "Prison Guard," 2014

of fraudsters are—the first answer is almost always the same: mailboxes! Wrong. Mailboxes aren't nearly as big of a target as people seem to think they are. Aside from the occasional W2, very few pieces of mail contain sensitive personal information. If a fraudster were to go through every mailbox looking for those gemstone envelopes, it would take forever. Then, people think about hackers.

On this count, our room full of people is right. Hackers are smart and efficient, and are way ahead of us. More than likely, they have already exposed your personal information, and this is where it all begins.

Hackers, program developers for information grabbers, and phishing scam operators are the criminals who fall under the **white-collar identity fraud** category. These people are highly skilled, sophisticated computer programmers, and as the Social Security Administration estimates, few and far between. The Administration believes there are *fewer than three hundred real hackers* that are of real concern. While there aren't many of them, they are of great concern, because these are the people who **expose** your information. Exposure is a key word for understanding how identity fraud is perpetrated. Just because your information has been exposed does not necessarily mean that it has been used or sold, although it could have been. At this point, every single American's identity has been exposed.

These three hundred hackers are more than likely the ones who are responsible for the data breaches that have dominated headlines for the past several years. In 2014, we've experienced what experts from the IT company Unisys (UIS) are calling "data-breach fatigue."[7] We've seen so many mass data breach stories that they no longer strike a strong chord with us. Their researchers compiled the following list of massive data breaches:

---

[7] Pagliery, "Half of American Adults Hacked This Year," 2014

- 76 million households affected by JP Morgan data breach
- 70 million Target customers' information (40 million credit and debit cards)
- 45 million TJ Maxx credit and debit cards
- 3.8 million filers in a state Department of Revenue data breach
- 33 million Adobe user credentials, and 3.2 million stolen credit and debit cards
- 4.6 million Snapchat users' account data
- 3 million payment cards used at Michaels stores
- 4.5 million Community Health Systems hospital records exposed[8]
- 1.1 million cards from Neiman Marcus
- "A significant number" of AOL's 120 million account holders
- Potentially all of eBay's 148 million customers' credentials
- 21.5 million identities from the Office of Personnel Management. Of that, 19.7 million were people applying for jobs requiring a security clearance.
- 32 million accounts stolen from Ashley Madison, a dating website for married individuals[9]

Often these hackers are offshore, from China, Russia, the Ukraine and other international locations. Tracking them, arresting and prosecuting them is almost impossible. This is a topic that touches on national security and would require a second book. So we will just state that they are out there and it is a very serious issue.

Okay, so hackers, the white-collar criminals of identity fraud, are breaking into company and government databases in order to get people's information. But why? It doesn't seem all that profitable. Oh, but it is. These data files are the Lego blocks of fortune to a fraudster. Hacks expose your information, which can then be sold to pettier criminals at a hugely inflated price. People can buy your

[8] Pagliery, "Hospital Network Hacked, 4.5 Million Records Stolen," 2014
[9] Wired, "Hackers Finally Post Stolen Ashley Madison Data," 2015.

information on the black market, which is where the hackers' profits come from. Much of this activity occurs on the Dark Web, parts of the Internet that cannot be seen by search engines.

What is Your Personal Information Worth?	
Name, Social Security number, Address, and date of birth	$10 - $100
Name, Social Security number, Address, date of birth, and Medicare Information	$100 - $300
Fake License	$100 - $400
DMV Driver's License	$300 - $4,500
Social Security Card	$500
Full information packet - Medicare number - Fake license - Fake Social Security card - Fake birth certificate	$1,400
Full information packet - Real identity, including -Legitimate state drivers license with a photo of the fraudster -Social Security card and number that matches -A real birth certificate	$7,500 - $12,500

Figure 1: These prices are for quantity one. Basic identity information in volume can drop well below $.50 for each identity. It becomes pretty evident that fraud is a growth industry for white-collar and blue-collar fraudsters. It's spiraling into a massive black market industry, with unimaginable profit and very small risk factors.[10]

Hackers expose and sell, so what exactly do all the other fraudsters do? While there is not much you, as an individual, can do to stop these white-collar hackers, you can do something to stop the **blue-collar identity thieves.** If their white-collar counterparts are the inventors, they are the innovators. Blue-collar identity fraud has a very low barrier to entry.

If someone explained the ins and outs of it to you, frankly, you

---

[10] These numbers were compiled from numerous Fraud of the Day articles.

could quit your job and start tomorrow. As security specialist Gunter Ollmann put it, "Interested in credit card theft? There's an app for that." Ollmann was referring specifically to an online program developed in 2011 called Zeus, which was designed for inexperienced hackers to steal everything from credit card information to documents pertaining to homeland security. The app made it so anyone with an iPhone could steal your identity while using public Internet access. Checking your bank account while grabbing a coffee? Bad idea.

Even if a potential fraudster doesn't have a healthy black market connection, or a smartphone, there are still plenty of places where they can access personal information. Any office that uses paper documents, documents with your information on them, is a target for fraudsters. Where are people getting these forms? Tax preparation offices, accountant firms, banks, postal offices, healthcare officers, college and school buildings, government offices, and your own home. You would never imagine your babysitter stealing your identity, but it happens. All of these places contain your personal information, stored either on a computer system or in a filing cabinet—which are often left unlocked. All it takes is for one clever person, a secretary, a nurse, a custodian, a patient, to grab one form or just take a picture, and your identity is out the door. While this seems like it would be a minor occurrence, this form of identity fraud is one of the most worrisome. It is easy, non-aggressive, and accessible to almost everyone. By using the information found on a very basic form from any number of offices, health care buildings, or educational institutions, someone can fill out a tax return in your name, change the address, and start raking in the dough.

WHY FRAUD?

This is by far the easiest question we have to answer in this book. People commit identity fraud because it is *so easy to do*. In 2012, an unemployed woman used the Turbo Tax preparation program to file a return reporting that she earned over $3 million during the previous fiscal year. According to her tax return, the state government kept $2.1 million, implying that the state kept 65 percent of her income. She then requested a refund of $2.1 million. And then: She got it, no questions asked, paid out on a pre-paid debit card! The fraudster supposedly went on a $150,000 shopping spree over the course of three months after being awarded a debit card with her government refund. The most mystifying part of the story, in all honesty, is the fact that she bought a *used* van with the debit card.

The woman was only caught after she claimed to have lost the first debit card and applied for a second one. Think of all the used vans she could have bought with four million dollars! This woman did not even need to steal a pre-existing identity, she merely altered her own. She didn't have to change her name, her address, or even her Social Security number—she merely rewrote her total income.

According to an official at the Oregon Department of Revenue, the enormous claim triggered a flag on the return. Apparently, several individuals reviewed the document, and every one of them approved it.[11] "We do not have that many $2.1 million refund claims," the official said. "It absolutely should have been caught and was not." If this woman hadn't tried for a second card, she would still be walking around with $2.1 million in her pocket. The fact that one fraudulent tax return can yield such a loss of government funds is unbelievable. Government agencies need to step up their game in order to compete with the individuals trying to steal from them.

So fraud is easy. It's also lucrative. Government benefits can be worth more than many people realize, and we will discuss them more in the next chapter. But to fully understand *why* people fraud, it's important to realize that often, they're doing it to acquire government benefits. Benefits = money. More benefits = more money.

---

[11] Roberts, 2012

More identities that allow you to apply for more benefits = even more money.

Just as committing the fraud itself is easy, so too is getting the tools you need. Since criminals have realized the massive potential and profit from identity theft for the purpose of fraudulently claiming government benefits, the black market has responded in full. Small pieces of personal information, on average, can sell from $12-16.[12] For the price of a burger and a beer, someone can buy an identity, and use it for years to come, making hundreds of thousands of dollars in the process. In the last five years, Social Security numbers have become so easy to obtain that thieves now usually bundle the number with extra identifying information like birth dates and even medical records in order to jack up the price. Social Security numbers have become a commodity to buy and sell, and make an absolute killing off. For identity thieves, business is *good*.

Government benefits are a really wonderful thing in theory. Benefits for single parents, for the disabled, for veterans and for the elderly help the people who need it most. The problem is that a large percentage of these benefits are going to the wrong people. Millionaires getting Food Stamps? Don't laugh, it's happening. One lottery winner simply left his winnings off of his food stamp application form, remained eligible for the benefits, and continued using them after he won $2 million from the television show "Make Me Rich!" in June 2010.

There has always been fraud in government programs. What's different now is that fraudsters, equipped with the volume of information provided by the hackers, have latched onto government benefits and are applying for them in droves. People have come to understand, that, if they play their cards right, they can work government agencies in a way to provide themselves with hefty incomes. So far, the rationale behind committing identity fraud is looking

---

[12] Davis, 2013

pretty good. It's really easy to do. You can make a large profit selling the information. Or, if you want, you can file for government benefits, another source of profits. On top of this, right now, fraud is a low-risk crime. Of course, all the stories that we report on in this book come from fraudsters who have been caught, but what about the multitudes of fraudsters, or potential fraudsters, who are stealing money that we have no idea about?

HOW MUCH FRAUD IS HAPPENING?

How is this kind of governmental abuse measured? And more importantly, how is it not measured? The Federal Trade Commission (FTC) tracks identity theft. The FTC's mission is the promotion of consumer protection and the elimination and prevention of business practices that remove competition from the equation, such as coercive monopoly. The FTC garners its statistical analysis based on consumer complaints. This is both good and bad. The FTC provides a platform for victims of identity theft to come to and voice their complaints, and takes that abuse into account when compiling information. The problem lies in the fact that *most victims of identity theft do not know that they are victims.* How would a 6 year old know if their identity had been stolen? If the victims don't know there's a problem, they can't report it, thus making it virtually impossible to have any sure statistics and numbers for fraudulent activity. But as far as the *reported* FTC complaints go, for the last 14 years, identity theft has topped the list as the number one consumer complaint.

**Consumer Sentinel Network
Complaint Type Count[1]
Calendar Years 2001 through 2014**

| Calendar Year | Consumer Sentinel Network Complaint Count | | | |
	Fraud	Identity Theft	Other	Total Complaints
2001	137,306	86,250	101,963	325,519
2002	242,783	161,977	146,862	551,622
2003	331,366	215,240	167,051	713,657
2004	410,298	246,909	203,176	860,383
2005	437,585	255,687	236,042	909,314
2006	423,672	246,234	236,243	906,129
2007	505,563	259,314	305,570	1,070,447
2008	626,832	314,587	325,705	1,261,124
2009	708,783	278,360	441,836	1,428,977
2010	828,072	251,074	399,160	1,478,306
2011	1,041,228	279,193	577,804	1,898,225
2012	1,113,298	369,143	630,420	2,112,861
2013	1,235,503	290,099	668,961	2,174,563
2014	1,554,860	332,646	695,345	2,582,851

[1] Complaint counts from CY-2001 to CY-2009 represent historical figures as per the Consumer Sentinel Network's five-year data retention policy. These complaint figures exclude National Do Not Call Registry complaints.

Federal Trade Commission　　　　Page 3 of 102　　　　Released February 2015

Figure 2: FTC complaint history from 2001-2014.

In 2001 the FTC's statistics showed identity theft accounting for 26 percent of all consumer complaints, or 86,000 claimed stolen identities. In 2001, collecting this information was relatively new for the FTC, as identity theft simply had not been a major problem until then. In 2012, complaints had increased to 369,145. This is all of the identity theft complaints from across the nation.

Yet, consider what the Treasury Inspector General for Tax Administration (TIGTA) tells us about the amount of fraud they are encountering. The TIGTA helps regulate the mass numbers of tax returns and refunds that the IRS distributes each year. The organization calls identity fraud the "crime of the 21st century."[13] Though the exact numbers are unknown, identity fraud rates are going up. In 2011, the IRS identified over one million incidents of identity theft. In 2012, it rose to 1.8 million, and by 2013, it had risen to 2.5 million. That's an incredible increase, and it occurred in only a few

---

[13] From "The Top Ten Scams Targeting Seniors," by the National Council on Aging, as cited by the Honorable J. Russell George in his "Tax-Related Identity Theft: An Epidemic Facing Seniors and Taxpayers"

years. Because people are not getting caught doing it, and because there is little being done to stop it people do not feel as if they will get caught, and for the most part, they're right.

All of these factors, ease, profit, government benefits, low risk, and low level of accountability, lead us to the findings of several government reports. The TIGTA report notes the same thing that the Federal Trade Commission does: identity fraud is increasing, and at rates that we do not even know about. What these numbers can tell us, aside from the sheer number of fraudsters out there, is that the "Why Fraud?" question is irrelevant. What people seem to be asking themselves now is "Why *Not* Fraud?"

The difference between the FTC's numbers and the TIGTA report indicates to us a massive discrepancy between what's being reported and the real number. The holes in this reporting system are huge. Let's remember that the FTC statistics are only registered complaints. If you live in New York and someone uses your identity to get food stamps—also known as SNAP benefits—or unemployment benefits in California, will California call you and let you know? Unfortunately not. This pattern follows for all types of government benefits: Housing, WIC (Women, Infants, and Children), Welfare, TANF (Temporary Assistance to Needy Families), Worker's Compensation, and the list goes on. There are a plethora of programs at the state and federal levels that will never notify the true owner of an identity that their identity may have been compromised. Therefore, the victim, not knowing that they are in fact a victim, will not report the incident.

Estimates of unregistered identity thefts are difficult to tabulate. We've attempted to quantify the problem by using a GAO report.[14]

The GAO estimates that there were about 16 million identity thefts. Based on the FTC complaint data, we have extrapolated and figure that for every registered complaint of identity theft reported to

---

[14] Bureau of Justice Statistics, 2013

the FTC, (shown in the chart above) approximately 36 unregistered identity thefts actually take place. Meaning it's a 1:36 complaint to theft ratio.[15]

Regardless of which statistic you use, the growth in this area of identity theft is enormous. So if your brain cells (or what's left of them) have not totally abandoned ship from the onslaught of statistics you've just read (or skipped), keep in mind *why you should care*. Identity theft is a lot bigger and badder than even our numbers know.

How Fast Is Identity Theft Growing? Various Government Agencies' Perspectives

2001-2004
2001: New York State reported 7,000 identity thefts
2004: New York State reported 17,600 identity thefts[16]

2009-2011
Taxpayer requests for help during this period rise by 142 percent[17]

---

[15] This is an approximation by the statistics contained in the GAO report from 2009
[16] In 2005, Federal and State laws restricted use of Social Security numbers, yet gaps remain
[17] Journal of Accountancy, 2012

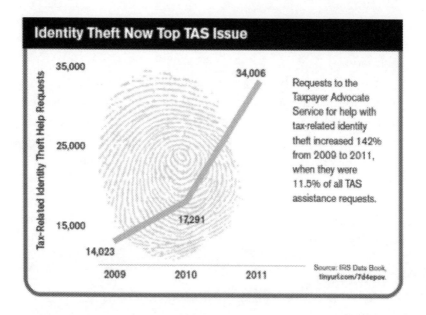

Figure 3: Identity theft has seen a surge of cases, with a 97 percent increase from 2010 to 2011.

2011-2012[18]
2011: Determined 940,000 fraudulent tax returns
2012: Determined 1,790,000 fraudulent tax returns,

2013 Bureau of Justice:
16.6 million adults who experienced identity theft

2012-2013[19] **Student fraud rings**
Student Aid Fraud Rings are estimated to have grown 82 percent, causing $187 million in losses to the Department of Education, most examples tied to identity theft.

---

[18] George, 2013
[19] Tighe, 2013

IDENTITY FRAUD – THE GREAT ENABLER

Fraud pays the bills for criminals, it's true, but it's not just about the money. Possessing someone else's identity enables even more serious crimes than theft. "Anyone who fraudulently obtains a genuine government ID may pose a threat to public safety,' says Bruce M. Foucart, the special agent in charge of Homeland Security Investigations, Boston.

The Center for Identity Management and Information Protection performed a comprehensive analysis on 517 identity theft cases investigated by the United States Secret Service between 2000 and 2006, and found that counterfeit drivers' licenses were used in 35 percent of these cases.

With 16 million stolen identities, per the DOJ, assume that 35 percent involve a fraudulent license. That would yield 5.6 million fraudulent licenses kicking around. With 210 million licensed drivers in the United States, 5.6 million fraudulent licenses would represent 2.6 percent of the outstanding licenses. You think this is crazy? Perhaps just too many to be possible? Now consider that on average 22 percent of the 20 million college students have fake id's, that's 4.4 million licenses alone.[20] Now go online and see how many websites offer fake license services.

If an illegal alien obtains an identity, he or she has the ability to apply for a license and passport, open bank accounts, apply and qualify for government and student loans, purchase property and vehicles, get a credit card, and of course, apply for government benefits. The documents allow fraudsters to impersonate a person online and in real life. If someone steals your identity, they can use that information to obtain a driver's license with your name, and their picture. This opens up a whole raft of possibilities, from getting a job as an illegal immigrant, to a worst-case scenario of terrorist acts.

[20] Martinez, Rutledge, and Sher. "Fake ID Ownership and Heavy Drinking in Underage College Students."July 16, 2009

The terrorist attacks of September 11th, 2001, were fully enabled by identity theft. When the 9/11 Commission Report was published, only 10 pages—starting with page 39—were devoted to suggestions for dealing with the deeply connected problems of terrorism and identity fraud. Yet, "travel documents are as important as weapons," the report says. "Fraud is no longer just a problem of theft. At many entry points to vulnerable facilities, including gates for boarding aircraft, sources of identification are the last opportunity to ensure that people are who they say they are." Not surprisingly, there has been little federal movement to work towards eradicating, or even minimizing, fraud and identity theft.

Judith Collins, an identity theft expert and professor we know at Michigan State University, worries that "It's going to take somebody who's really going to be married to this issue in terms of some knowledge and ability and skills and devotion and strict focus on this one single issue, and I don't know who would do it."[21] This is one of the reasons we've written this book: We don't think it can single-handedly spur people to take the actions necessary to stop identity theft and control identity fraud, but we hope it serves as a wake-up call.

Proper documentation for American citizens is a difficult problem to tackle. Strategies for fixing this widespread issue are being put into place in Departments of Motor Vehicles across the country—something that will be discussed in a later chapter. However, a report from the United States Government Accountability Office (GAO) anticipates that the problem with identity documentation will not be fixed until 2023.[22]

Some states are choosing not to comply or cooperate with other states by sharing information, difficulties (technological and otherwise) detecting forged birth certificates, and validating legitimate dates of birth. Most of these problems are a firsthand result of inaccurate and incomplete data submitted to states and their agencies

---

[21] Sullivan, 2004
[22] United States Government Accountability Office, 2012

from websites requesting self-reported information. The Act that the document proposes is slowly being implemented, but we're getting ahead of ourselves. In late 2015, that means they are anticipating a little over seven years before this is under control. That's seven more years of enablement that potential fraudsters can take advantage of, and possibly already have.

In fact, in almost every case that we're aware of, agencies and states are refusing to share information with each other, because legally they aren't permitted to do it. If they disseminate their information to another government body, they could be liable for a data breach. And, of course, there are political reasons to remain in control of your own information.

WHO IS HURT MOST?

There are certain groups of people who, as you can imagine, are more often targeted for identity theft. The deceased, severely handicapped, prisoners, elderly living in or out of retirement homes, Puerto Ricans and other citizens of U.S. territories, and kids are all major targets. Senior citizens are most likely to have a 'nest egg', to own their home as opposed to renting, and/or have excellent credit. Often, seniors are not checking their credit and Social Security number as closely as the rest of us, and generally have less awareness when it comes to the hazards of the Internet and what personal information you should keep off the web.

One recent survey from the FTC found that 87 percent of consumers had been asked for either all or part of their Social Security number within the past year. Seventy-eight percent of those surveyed indicated that they would prefer not to provide their Social Security number, but were concerned about their ability to obtain services if they failed to do so.[23] With this type of perceived pressure, seniors, who have learned to give out their Social Security number when

---

[23] Federal Trade Commission, 2007

asked, will relent and give their number in order to get the needed services or products, thus expanding their electronic footprint and exposing them to additional risk of identity theft. Senior citizens often do not report if their identity has been compromised, and even if they do, the cases can be difficult to prosecute, and are considered a low-risk crime.[24]

Kids' identities are a fraudster's best friend. Kids start with a clean history; what kid do you know who's deep in candy bar debt? Kids' identities are not usually monitored by their parents, and can be used, undetected, for years before anyone notices that the little tyke has a driver's license and just got a loan for his new yacht. In many cases, identity theft is due to Friendly Fraud, meaning mom and dad are in on it, and using poor Billy's identity for their own purposes, like using his identity as their own to escape their debt. In the Carnegie Mellon study of compromised children's identities found that over 10 percent of children's identities have been stolen or used. Therefore, 7.6 million stolen identities are not being reported until these kids become adults and try and qualify for loans or credit. The study found that a child's identity is *51 times more likely to be stolen than an adult's*—think about it. Do you have kids? When was the last time you checked on their identities?

One particularly heart-wrenching story of identity fraud is that of a college student who attempted to apply for her first credit card during her freshman year. The first credit card company she applied to rejected her, as did the second. She soon discovered that someone had stolen her identity and had run up massive debt—a debt of $1.5 million. Apparently, the crime had started when she was only nine. Someone had stolen her Social Security number and set up false identities and more than 42 accounts. The student still faces being rejected if she applies for a credit card or student loan or tries to rent a car or a house.

---

[24] George, 2013

"We've seen children have this crime begin as early as 5 months old and then it goes on for years," said Bo Holland, founder and CEO of All Clear ID, a company that offers basic identity theft protection to consumers.

"A parent will typically find out when their child is moving into adulthood," Holland added. "When they are about to go to college, they apply for that first loan and, boom, they get denied." Holland also noted how parents can be fooled into thinking their children's identities are protected: "They'll use your child's Social Security number with a different name and a different birth date," Holland said. "So if you pull a credit report, the credit report is looking for a specific name and the birthday that goes with it. And so you won't find it. You'll get "file not found," and you'll feel safe." David Vladeck, the FTC's director of the Bureau of Consumer Protection puts identity theft in a truly clear light: "It's undetected and undetectable."

Children who are victims of identity theft from a young age are usually not part of the FTC annual statistics, and they will not be recognized as victims for years to come. Another common target of thieves are identities stolen from Puerto Rico that are being used in the United States to submit fraudulent tax returns to the IRS. Citizens of Puerto Rico do not pay taxes to the IRS, but to the Puerto Rican tax authority. Since Puerto Rico is a U.S. territory, all citizens get a Social Security number from the Social Security Administration. Therefore all Social Security numbers from Puerto Rico that are submitted to the Social Security Administration are real, and it is assumed that the individual has simply relocated. Large quantities of Puerto Rican identities have shown up all over the country requesting refunds.

Perhaps you're thinking that if your identity had been stolen, you would have heard about it, right? Not really. The Open Security Foundation states that over 867 million identities were stolen from 2005 to 2013. Based on the FTC statistics we mentioned earlier,

27,000 identities are reported stolen every day. If you do the math, you realize that it's statistically improbable that your identity hasn't already been stolen—multiple times.

After a large-scale data breach, most companies will get everyone whose personal information was compromised credit protection for 12 months. After the 12 months, some people will start paying for the credit protection on their own, but many will get comfortable, and let it lapse. These individuals figure that if someone hasn't started using their identity now, that they'll simply get lost in the shuffle, maybe the fraudsters will forget about it, or lose it. But fraudsters know all about this, and they will start using stolen identities after a few years, to better ensure that credit protection won't flag criminal activity. Think of your identity as a fine wine. The older it becomes after theft, the less likely it is to be protected, thus the more valuable it becomes. Even if your identity has not been used today, it's pretty safe to say that it will be used in time to come.

HOW MUCH DOES FRAUD COST US?

Every agency uses the same caveat: Its numbers are estimates and no one really knows the actual amount of fraud. But we have estimated a number, and we are going to share our methodology with you. We have extrapolated our estimates on a) the overall amount of estimated fraud from each agency and b) created an estimate of *identity fraud* used to defraud that agency. As an example, tax refund fraud is 100% tied to identity fraud. Now consider Medicare or Medicaid. Both of these programs can be defrauded in many ways that don't even use or need false identities. We know that identity theft and fraud are taking place with healthcare and we have trended this across the multitude of Fraud of the Day articles to develop our estimate of these programs at 5% tied to identity fraud. So by knowing the agency reported fraud and multiplying by the percent that uses identities to defraud that agency, we can get an estimate. We will take the same position that our number is an estimate. We believe it is very low, but no one knows the true level of fraud in these programs.

Fraud In Major Agencies - 2014

Medicare: $60 billion
Medicaid: $17.7 billion
IRS (Tax Refund Fraud): $5.2 billion
IRS (Earned Income Tax Credit Fraud): $14.5 billion
SSA: $4.3 billion
Student loans: $1 billion
Unemployment: $6.2 billion
SNAP: $1billion

Our estimate of the total fraud at the major agencies, based on the reports we've been tracking, is $109.9 billion. Now the question is what percentage is tied to identity theft? Here are our estimates.

Medicare: 5%
Medicaid: 5%
IRS: (Tax Refund Fraud): 100%
IRS: (Earned Income Tax Credit Fraud) 100%
SSA: 15%
Student loans: 70%
Unemployment: 15%
SNAP: 10%

We estimated fraud in the other programs, including housing, home heating fuel, cell phones, FEMA, head start programs and rental assistance at $1 billion.

Our conclusion: The federal and state governments are losing $26.87 billion a year to identity-theft based fraud, about a quarter of fraud across major agencies of $109.9 billion. We believe that the government can save taxpayers billions of dollars, and save many of us from experiencing identity theft, by reforming the application process for benefits.

How to Fraud 101: Student Loans

As with most forms of identity fraud, we'll need lots of identities, a laptop, and Internet access. Committing fraud, regardless of what type, requires only a few key ingredients.

We'll focus on applying for Pell Grants, federal need-based student grants, as they never need to be paid back. Since these programs are not looking for a return check, it is less likely that they will check on their recipient, keeping them from knowing the truth about where their money went. After we apply for grants, then we go for the loans. Loans are good, but when the agency seeks out the frat boy whose identity we stole, they'll start looking for a trail to follow back to us. Lesson? Grants are better than loans. And in 2014-2015, you can get Pell Grants of $5,730 each.

Our first step will be to submit FASFA applications to the Department of Education. We'll claim a very modest income, several dependents who live at the home address, and only a few assets (go for the bike instead of the car!). This is no different from tax refund fraud; very little information is checked or verified, so if we have any applications that are stopped or not accepted, we don't even call in. We'll just fill out another application with a new name and identity. Lastly, if they are starting to smarten up and start checking IP addresses, we need to walk over to an apartment complex or an Internet café and pump out the paperwork through some open WIFI connections.

We'll be sure to mix and match our identities. John Smith,

with Tim Bishop's Social Security number and Beth Jones's address, with a made up date of birth just to keep them on their toes. That way, if and when the companies that gave out the student loans come looking to collect, no one who can be held accountable—because no one under that name, Social Security number, address, and date of birth exists.

Our last step will be to hire a few kids to pose as the student, attend the first one or two classes, and then drop the class online. Or, if we're lucky, the class is held online and we can log in once, say, "This class isn't for me," and ask for a refund. After we "drop out," we'll receive 100 percent of the value of the course in cash.

CHAPTER TWO

How Fraudsters Fraud: The Information Gold Mine

The U.S. Federal Government runs a web site called Benefits.gov, which helps people figure out which state and federal benefits they are eligible for and how to apply. But the site tries to make it clear that government benefits are for people in specific circumstances, not just anybody. "Many people arrive at Benefits.gov after seeing unofficial advertisements that might have them thinking that the government will give "free money" to essentially *anyone* for *anything*. The government will not give you money just because you ask for it," reads one paragraph on the site.

Unfortunately, this isn't really true. The government is giving lots of people money, identity fraudsters in particular, just because they ask for it.

Good benefits are going to bad people, and ruining it for everyone. Fraudsters stealing government benefits are not just stealing from the people who actually need it, but they're stealing from you as well! If you pay tax dollars, then you might have just bought your neighborhood fraudster a new yacht. One couple in Florida lived on a yacht while collecting welfare and Food Stamps. The husband was the chief executive officer of a satellite television and broadband services company and his wife bred and sold championship dogs. Over seven years the couple deposited $2.6 million in bank accounts, which they conveniently forgot to mention on their public assistance applications. To say the least, these two were not strapped for cash.

How did it happen that two yacht-owning wealthy people can bilk U.S. taxpayers for millions of dollars for years and not get caught for seven years? The answer lies in the fact that Americans' most important form of identification, our Social Security cards and our drivers' licenses, are issued using systems that weren't great to begin with -- and whose holes are now painfully obvious as more of our lives are moving online.

The fundamental building block of our identity is the infamous Social Security number. It's infamous to people who care about secure identities, anyway. From 1946 to 1972 each printed Social Security card read, "Not For Identification."

But didn't you just say our Social Security number was our identity? When did that change?

Well apparently, our government used to be smarter. The Social Security Administration noted that your Social Security number and the Social Security card should not be used for identification because it has no photograph, physical description, or birth date. Seems pretty obvious, right?

Figure 4: An example of a pre-1972 Social Security card. Note the "NOT FOR IDENTIFICATION" emblazoned in all capital letters at the bottom.

Oddly enough, nothing has changed since then. Our Social Security cards still lack the critical information that turns a nine-digit number into an individual. All our Social Security cards do is confirm that the number shown is associated with the name printed on the card. But in the past, since the majority of Americans held a Social Security card in their wallets, all of the other agencies began using it as the primary way to track citizens. Therefore, in 1972 the Social Security Administration removed the "Not for Identification" statement from the cards. Today the Social Security number is frequently used as an authenticator for critical tracking and identification. Banks, insurance companies, government benefits agencies, and state and federal taxes are all tightly united by an individual's Social Security number for identification and tracking purposes. This is a *terrible* idea. Using the Social Security number without other verified documentation is just a recipe for fraud and deception.

For the most common fraud schemes, there are only two main ingredients for claiming benefits. A name and Social Security number can provide fraudsters with incredible access to your information. An address and date of birth in addition create an absolute gold mine. Together, they form the pieces of a puzzle that opens many other doors. Can't remember your bank account password? No problem then, what's your birthday? Or the last four digits of your Social Security number? Bingo. These pieces of information can be combined, flipped, and changed in so many combinations and variations, many of which are workable, fraudable amalgamations. If you just have a Social Security number, maybe one bought on the Dark Web, you can fraud. If you have a name, you can fraud. If the name and Social Security number match, *awesome*. Hmmm… what's a good address? 33 Fraudster Lane? Sounds legitimate! Can you make up a birthday? How's March 15th? Clearly, the government is going to miss the Julius Caesar reference.

Any hopes of change on the horizon? As we were writing this book, a new project being run by the Social Security Administration was announced.

"To reduce the number of replacement card requests in field offices and card centers, the Social Security Administration is developing an Internet-based Social Security number Replacement Cards (iSSNRC) application, which will allow American citizens who meet certain criteria to request replacement cards online by completing an application and providing data from your state issued drivers license or ID Card."[25] If you read between the lines, you'll realize that this application actually will increase the number of replacement card requests, because fraudsters now will be able to request them online. Now, you can buy an illegal identity, or steal one yourself, with a corresponding drivers license number and use that to apply for a Social Security replacement card online.[26]

This is perhaps one of the worst ideas in history. (OK, we're

---

[25] United States Government Accountability Office, 2012
[26] Tighe, 2013

biased, because we care so much about identity theft, but it is a truly bad idea).

TYPES OF IDENTITY THEFT

The stories that come out of fraud run the gamut from the sad and pathetic to the sick and twisted. One of our favorites is of the man who dressed up as his deceased mother for six years in order to keep claiming her benefits. This guy went all out: wig, make-up, cane, even an oxygen tank. You have to give him points for creativity at the very least. The fraudster apparently gave the funeral director the wrong Social Security number and date of birth for his mother so that her death would not be registered in government databases. After making sure her death would not be accurately recorded, he began collecting $700 a month in Social Security in her name, in addition to his own disability checks. He repeatedly cashed in his dead mother's payments and collected the rent subsidies on the $2.2 million Brooklyn apartment she had left him. The man's mother, an actress, died in September 2003. However, the woman's monthly benefits were paid until June 2009. Along with the real estate fraud, the man and his partner cashed his mother's social security checks every month for six years, stealing about $115,000 in all.[27]

The fraudster was eventually caught when he sought out prosecutors, dressed up in his full disguise, to complain he was being ripped off by the man who bought the apartment for $660,000 in a foreclosure auction. We can imagine the moment of reveal was very dramatic, when the little old lady with smeared lipstick and a bad perm turned out to be a middle-aged, pasty white dude. Can you imagine what the prosecutors thought? *Her hands did look a little beefy now that I think about it...*

These stories are crazy, unimaginable, and sometimes pretty

---

[27] Daily News, "Man who 'dressed up as his mother for six years to steal $115,000 in benefits' faces 25 years in prison, 2012."

hilarious. The fraudsters are endlessly inventive: blocked from one kind of fraud, they can easily turn to another. We've identified at least five different categories of identity theft. The most common is "true name" identity theft, which is very common -- and which basically means stealing a stranger's identity. But you can also modify your own identity, say by making yourself older to claim Social Security. You can create a synthetic identity, fully or partially (more on that later). You can also use a relative's identity, such as that of your parent who has passed, or a living child, with or without permission. And you can use someone else's identity, with his or her permission, such as a prisoner or a homeless woman who sells or loans her identity.

ORGANIZED IDENTITY FRAUD

Organized identity fraud crime, like any other organized crime, can run the gamut from two individuals conspiring together to a massive network of criminals working in several countries. Organized fraudsters could include some of those special 300 (remember the real hackers from Chapter One, the people who can hack large-scale business and government databases and distribute and expose individuals' personal information?), or fraudsters capable of developing **phishing scams**. Phishing scams involve posing as a legitimate organization's website or email, wherein you'll receive an email claiming you've won a prize or that Amazon.com needs to verify your personal information. You might fill it out, thinking nothing of it, and end up giving your personal details to a fraudster.

Organized identity fraudsters target corporations and institutions, but government agencies are the big game of the data breach world. There's a lot more than money at stake.

Take this example: In 2012, a phishing email was sent to multiple Department of Revenue employees. At least one of them clicked on the link, triggering the embedded malware. The malware stole the user's username and password. Two weeks later, the attacker logged in using a remote access service with the stolen credentials. The attacker then began installing some password-grabbing utilities, later using the obtained passwords to connect to more servers. Throughout the propagation process, the attacker used some generic database client software to search for interesting data. One month after the initial infection, the attacker found worthy loot: a Department of Revenue database backup. It took the attacker *two days* to copy the 74GB database, and send it, via another server within the victim's internal network, to the attacker's servers. This was pretty much the last contact the attacker had with its target. Two months after the initial infection, and one month after the attacker had finished extracting the desired information, the Secret Service informed the Department of Revenue of the breach. Needless to say, the Department of Revenue "had no idea what had happened."[28]

One kind of phishing scam that is emerging globally are fake websites that mimic official, government websites. The United Kingdom is having significant problems with this, along with Canada, and most likely, many other countries that have not yet discovered government web sites that have false counterparts. In the United States, there is a fake site that mirrors the IRS's official website, except with a .com instead of a *.gov* at the end. There are even fake websites that have obtained a .org domain, which even the most prudent of skeptics might miss when keying in their personal information.

These fake sites may try emailing or texting their victims to 'confirm personal information,' a tagline that has led many into a trap. Other forms of organized fraud include focused hiring and keystroke grabbing. In focused hiring, a receptionist or janitor will be hired having already been prepped by the fraudsters to photograph or copy down information from medical or tax forms. Using a keystroke grabber program, someone, often someone working in

---

[28] Be'ery, 2012

an office, can insert a USB drive into a computer, where it can't be seen, to record all of the keystrokes that happened in the course of a day, i.e., passwords. These are not nearly all of the schemes concocted by fraudsters, and there are more developing daily.

Often, internal involvement is crucial for these operations to be successful. Having someone on the inside is incredibly valuable.

One such large-scale operation not only put dangerous drivers on the streets, but also created a jumping-off point for other criminal activity. A Chinatown license fraud ring involved four crooked Secretary of State Office employees and potentially dozens of other participants. They confirmed to the FBI that as many as 8,000 people obtained Illinois drivers licenses and state IDs through the ring.[29]

Those licenses were sold to illegal aliens and criminals so they could use the identities of legitimate Illinois citizens. And now what can those illegal aliens and criminals do with their newfound proof of identity? Why, they can apply for benefits, evade state and federal level law enforcement and punishment, and apply for other forms of identification. And what happens to those citizens who have had their identities compromised? Everything from credit card and bank loans made out in their names, to being turned down for a job, to having warrants issued for their arrest. In a few cases the victims were arrested for the crime committed by the fraudster, and they spent time in jail until their identity could be resolved.

WHY IS MORE GOVERNMENT FRAUD HAPPENING NOW?

The answer, in a nutshell, to why more government fraud is happening now, is technology. We're all putting more of our information online, where identity thieves can access it. More importantly, the government has transitioned to the online world in ways that have

---

[29] Chicago Sun-Times, "The Watchdogs: Chinatown license fraud ring put dangerous drivers on the street," 2012.

allowed identity thieves and fraudsters to perpetrate more fraud and scale the frauds they are perpetrating. In the pursuit of convenience and efficiency, government took away the safeguards against fraud. Mostly, the government has replaced human review of benefit applications with *no review at all.*

Since the Internet became something the average person could carry around in his or her pocket, there are more entry places for a fraudster, i.e., more smartphones, computers, and other Internet-capable devices. Often, these devices are portable, like laptops. Imagine each device as a revolving door: They continually swing open and shut, allowing the people who are looking for the opportunities to get inside more chances. Each time you log online and check any kind of personal account, you could be compromising your personal information. Now more than ever, people store and access their personal information online, and use multiple devices to check that information. Scores of people own a smartphone, and a laptop, and a tablet. Did Susan log out of her tax form on both her laptop and iPhone? Did Mike forget to sign off of his Social Security statement when his Facebook page distracted him? Rest assured, even if you didn't remember, the fraudsters who hack their way into your Wi-Fi connection most certainly did.

Widespread Internet use through multiple devices allows fraud; so does the more prevalent use of debit cards. Many government agencies use debit cards to give out government benefits, as they're more cost-effective and ensure more privacy for the user. Sending out pre-paid debit cards certainly has their advantages. Funds can be added to them, as opposed to cutting multiple checks and sending them out separately. The Americans who are unbanked and would normally have to pay high fees to check cashing locations, can use the debit cards instead. Individuals on benefit programs no longer have to feel embarrassed while they check out with what are obviously Food Stamp coupons. Now, those people can discreetly pay for their groceries just as anyone else would.

Unfortunately, these debit cards come with a raft of problems for government agencies. Cashing a check involves showing up to the bank, having a matching signature, and photo identification. With a debit card, all you have to do is go to the nearest ATM. Payments can also be electronically deposited into a bank account. The Federal Trade Commission's "Red Flags Rules" dictate that, at a minimum, a bank must verify that a name, address, and Social Security number match before an account can be created for that individual. That's all well and good, but even these verifications can easily be circumvented by simply getting an account in another name (with an identity that is not your own), and ensuring that deposits are sent to that account.

The IRS's lax practices exacerbate the situation, and the IRS, as we discussed in the last chapter, is one of the biggest targets of fraud. Currently, the IRS does not take even the basic step of verifying that the account it drops tax refunds into matches the name that they have on file. A report from a few years ago by the Inspector General for Tax Administration states:

> The IRS has not developed processes to ensure that the more than 61 million Filing Season 2008 tax refunds were deposited only to an account in the name of the filer, as required by Federal direct deposit regulations. Consequently, there is an increased risk of refund fraud as well as the potential that inadvertent errors can result in depositing refunds into the wrong bank account. [...] The IRS places responsibility for compliance with Federal direct deposit regulations on the taxpayer—indicating it is the taxpayer's responsibility to ensure that their tax refunds are only directly deposited into their accounts.[30]

---

[30] Phillips, 2008

Basically, if you have a false identity, it's a lot easier to access government benefits if they are issued by debit card rather than by a check. It's also easier to buy non-approved items with debit cards (like alcohol and cigarettes) than it is with Food Stamps. State-issued EBT cards—cards that work similarly to debit cards, except that they do not allow accessing cash—only allow the purchase of food items. This card is usually traded by fraudsters for 50 percent of the cash value held on the card. Often, these cards are purchased by storeowners who buy them with cash, and use the monetary balance to buy bulk items such as soda or candy for their own stores. Most EBT cards do not have any kind of photo identification on them, making it difficult to know if the person using the card is actually the person it was given to. Recipients also are able to call in state agencies roughly 10 times per year to claim a lost or stolen card before privileges are revoked.

Another reason for the explosion of fraud now is the indiscriminate requests by businesses and organizations for electronic and hardcopy records containing Personal Identifiable Information (PII), such as your Social Security number or birthday. Ever wonder why your chiropractor needed your Social Security number? Your number may have funded that fancy new BMW in the parking lot. This is not to say that every doctor, dentist, secretary, and custodian is out to get your personal information, but the reality of the situation is that some are, and that your identity can be stolen if it's out in the open, unprotected.

As recently as 15 years ago government programs only used the Internet to disseminate program information; no one applied for benefits online. Applicants and beneficiaries were still required to visit an office and show identification to apply and collect program benefits. Over the last decade, the Internet has become a way for agencies to cut labor costs, expand hours, and -- depending on whom you ask -- improve customer service. Conversely, this has made the application process and the collection of benefits an anonymous process, with the government's expectation that the self-reported information from the applicant is correct and accurate. Since these government agencies rely on self-reported data, people have been able to paint inaccurate pictures of themselves, putting on and taking off identities like pairs of pants.

Take Jill and Mike, who hid assets while pocketing welfare benefits. The advent of self-reported data has allowed Jill to have two Social Security numbers and a dozen aliases. Mike has eight aliases that are variations on his own name. Jill and Mike are married. Mike owns the house that he and Jill live in together, but Jill submits for housing subsidy under another identity. After three years, Mike sells the house and makes a profit of $110,000. At the same time, Jill buys another house under one Social Security number and files for housing subsidy on the same property using the other Social Security number. She then used her aliases and two Social Security numbers to receive the following benefits:

- $4,067 in Social Security disability payments
- $1,370 in food assistance benefits
- $995 in welfare benefits
- $756.13 in Medicaid payments
- $136,000 loan modification and $200,000 home equity loan, with her husband claiming to be her employer

The mixed picture of identities that Jill and Mike present to the government allows them to appear to be whomever they want. But how are they getting away with it? None of the agencies cross-referenced or verified the information the couple used. A lot of it -- like Jill's age -- could be entirely fabricated, meaning that she could claim various benefits.

Let's remember one of the most important lessons: most fraudsters are not stupid. They continually test systems to see where the holes and weaknesses are. If they manage to use a piece of information for one benefit, they may try for another, as the risk of being caught is so low. So when these criminals are hiding behind a computer screen, applying for benefits, their face does not even have to match that on the identification that they're using, because they're frauding from the comfort of their own home, watching Oprah and Leave It To Beaver reruns. Now there's convenience for you.

Another way that technology enables fraud: Home computers with fairly basic software allow the creation of high-quality fraudulent documentation. Birth certificates, utility bills, and even social security cards can be created. These documents are used to verify residency, address and identity. They are usually then used to get driver's licenses and or passports. How easy is it to get a fake driver's license? Visit nearly any college campus in the country and ask around. Though most of these undergrads only want to use them to get into the bars on dollar beer night, it goes to show just how easy it is to fabricate usable, "government-issued" forms of identification. And for the ones who are smart enough to use those new IDs for more than just boozing? Brand new, college-educated fraudsters.

WHAT DEFINES AN IDENTITY

The preference of many government agencies for self-reported data because of convenience and a smaller need for manpower is one of the biggest contributing factor to the explosion of fraud, but there are several other factors at work here as well. The next biggest hurdle is that identities are not static, but **dynamic**. When the government looks at an identity, they see first and foremost your Golden Four (name, address, Social Security number, and date of birth). Let's imagine a Ms. Elizabeth Tammy Baker as a single entity. She lives in Wisconsin. What happens when Ms. Elizabeth Tammy Baker gets married, and changes her name to Mrs. Elizabeth Tammy Young? Also, she just moved, out of state. So now we have a Mrs. Elizabeth Tammy Young in Missouri. What happened to Ms. Elizabeth Tammy Baker? Does that identity just disappear? What happens if Mrs. Elizabeth Tammy Young decides her name is too long and starts going by Mrs. Elizabeth T. Young, or just Mrs. Elizabeth Young? What if she wises up to the possibility that she has endless chances to reinvent herself? Here, this imaginary woman's identity has become *dynamic*. She took two key aspects of her Golden Four, her name and address, and changed them. The government has no ability to see that her identity has changed, has become dynamic. Over time, humans change. Our names change, our address changes. *Hold on,* you think, *what about your birthday? Or your Social Security number?* That *never changes.* Well, it's certainly not supposed to. But if you get a 'new' person in a new state, and a Social Security number with two flipped digits, and no one verifies it, a hole is made. Let's look at all the possible names that the original Ms. Elizabeth Tammy Baker could assume, with the variations on her original name on the left and their reincarnations on the right:

1. Elizabeth Tammy Baker	1. Elizabeth Tammy Young
2. Elizabeth T. Baker	2. Elizabeth T. Young
3. E. Baker	3. E. Young
4. E.T. Baker	4. E.T. Young
5. Lizz Baker	5. Lizz Young
6. Lizz T. Baker	6. Lizz T. Young
7. Lizz Tammy Baker	7. Lizz Tammy Young
8. Tammy Baker	8. Tammy Young
9. Tam Baker	9. Tam Young
10. Tamm Baker	10. Tamm Baker
11. Beth Baker	11. Beth Young
12. Beth T. Baker	12. Beth T. Young
13. Beth Tammy Baker	13. Beth Tammy Young

Figure 5: Reincarnations of one identity and its numerous possible spin-offs.

In addition to being dynamic, identities can also be **synthetic**, meaning that part, or all, of the identity can be made up. Often, the most successful synthetic identities are the ones that combine a matching name and Social Security number, as those are the two main pieces of information that are most likely to be checked. If the Social Security Administration verifies that a name and Social Security number match, often government agencies, such as the Department of Motor Vehicles, will get the go-ahead for distributing benefits, identification, etc. Though the name-Social Security number combo is pretty strong, so is just having a working Social Security number. Even if a Social Security number is paired with a totally different (or made up) name on a government application form, often, no red flags will be raised. Why? Because even that bare minimum of verification is sometimes not performed.

Names and Social Security numbers are routinely not checked for a match through several government agencies. Often, made-up birthdates and addresses are added to this new, synthetic "identity." But what happens when this identity begins to develop itself in the public sector? What happens when Allie Kinder (in real life, a five-year old girl who had to go to the doctor's about a bad case of chicken pox) starts paying utility bills? Opening bank accounts? This is what happens when a synthetic identity begins to gather steam. It develops itself so that they appear as a real person, making real-life transactions. The fake identity begins to look legitimate.

The plain old Social Security number-only tactic is sometimes even more dangerous to law-abiding citizens than an all-out identity theft. Synthetic identity theft creates a fragment, or sub-file, to your main credit file. A fragmented file refers to additional credit report information tied to your Social Security number, but someone else's name and address. Negative information entered in the fragmented file is then linked to you, but doesn't actually belong to you. If you have good credit but there is derogatory information in the fragmented file, it could negatively impact your ability to get credit. Since this type of identity theft does not affect your main credit file, it often doesn't hit your credit report; nor will a fraud alert or credit freeze help. This means it takes longer to find out you've been victimized, making it harder for you to clear your name. When the identity intruder makes a pile of debt and then disappears, the credit card companies will come calling.

In addition to being very difficult to detect for both you and the credit card companies, synthetic identities are very difficult for government agencies that are distributing benefits to parse out from the rest. The Social Security numbers are legitimate, and because there is little to no verification happening at the agency level, it leaves the door wide open for fraudsters to game the system. One felon took synthetic identity theft to a whole new level. He essentially created a small army of synthetic identities. With the fake identities he created, he formed fake companies, used his "army" to simulate fake customers who would then buy fake products and generate fake revenue. It was an outlandish plan, but it worked, long enough for the fraudster to withdraw almost $2 million that his fake companies had supposedly generated.

According to the Federal Trade Commission, synthetic identity theft is the fastest-growing type of identity fraud in America. The FTC estimated that it currently accounts for up to 85 percent of all identity fraud.

Government agencies also face an internal threat: Because the crime of identity theft is so much a crime of opportunity, and so often goes unpunished, government workers may use their access and privilege to begin working on their own behalf for profit. If a fraudster is on the inside, they can wreak unimaginable havoc: printing official documents and identification, verifying identities that don't match, and stealing other individuals' personal information to either use for fraudulent purposes or to sell on the black market. One such internal threat happened at the Massachusetts Registry of Motor Vehicles (RMV). A man who was presenting papers stating that he was a Puerto Rican citizen approached a woman employed there. He admitted to the papers being false, but said he would pay her $200 for each license she made using fake documents. The RMV employee agreed to the deal, and began issuing the fake driver's licenses. The fake licenses allowed the people to conceal their true identities—if they have an American drivers license; it makes it much easier to hide under a false name without getting caught.

An informant told investigators on the case about two people in New York who were charging $4,000 for the fraudulent licenses, meaning that the man leading the fraudulent activity was making $3,800 off each license, after paying the RMV employee her share. One of the people who had obtained a fraudulent license from this scheme was a previously deported aggravated felon who had come back into the country. This scheme was making money, allowing illegal immigrants the appearance of lawful immigration status because of their fraudulent documents, and it allowed a convicted felon who was *deported* to come back into the country. Internal threats are a huge challenge for the government. The RMV employee in this scenario did not take much convincing to accept some extra cash on the side. How can government agencies tighten their hiring laws if background checks provide no insight? Government workers who use their status can cause consequences that often they don't understand. They open doors for enablement, leading to any number of criminal activities.

How to Fraud 102: Unemployment Benefits

This time, we're going to focus on how to do a complex identity fraud. Let's say we're planning on hitting a state Unemployment Agency for unemployment benefits. An average unemployment check is around $300, and you can qualify for up to 26 weekly payments, meaning that if everything goes well, you can make up to $7,800. For this identity fraud to work it will cost more up-front, but don't worry, the payout is huge.

In this scenario, the government agency has what would generally be seen as a solid fraud prevention program. This agency has full-time fraud investigators, a strong rules-based fraud filter generating leads, and it even checks data with the Death Master File from the Social Security Administration (to confirm that the applicant is alive). The fraud prevention manager for this Unemployment Agency is successful at stopping a lot of fraud and because of this, senior management is very happy. Unfortunately, the fraud prevention manager is only looking for (and thus only detecting) the older fraud schemes like deceased applicants, or people currently employed at another company. The fraud prevention manager is not aware of the open back door to unemployment payments that identity fraud creates.

The first thing we need to do is to get our hands on 100 identities. Not just any 100 identities though. This time, they need to be out-of-state, preferably a state that's far away from where you're applying. That's because we don't want the fraud prevention manager to have these identities in his system anywhere. The agency just might have a rules-based fraud filter looking for a name and Social Security number to match someone already in the system. If the identities are in-state, then it is acceptable to use identities stolen from someplace like an orthodontist's office or old folks' home, since identities of kids and the elderly are unlikely to be currently working, and thus won't be in the system.

Our second step is to start a company. Don't get discouraged, starting a company is easy! Let's come up with a name. "ACME" is a good go-to, so we'll register it with the state Secretary of State. This will cost a couple of dollars (say $100) but just remember, the fraud will turn back a lot of revenue. Next, register ACME online with the state Department of Labor (DOL). Unemployment benefit payments (for real employees) are paid by legitimate companies every quarter. The state DOL receives these payments and can then track who is in the system and who qualifies for what benefits in the future. It is important to note that there is not an official from the state who checks and verifies companies that register and make payments. The data being submitted online and paid quarterly is all self-reported and other than the amounts being checked for calculation errors it is treated as true. This means that our fake company ACME can self-report lies to the DOL, and appear legitimate to the state.

ACME needs to make one quarterly payment for the 100 employees, but it does not need to make a full payment. The important action for the fraud to work is to get the false self-reported information of these 100 employees into the DOL databases. The DOL is a large multi-layered government bureaucracy with one division in charge of receiving payments from employers and another in charge of making payments to people. The fact that the employer payments to the DOL were not paid in full by ACME will not factor into the 100 applying for and getting paid benefits. The cost for getting these self-reported lies into the system is $10,000 (but could be done for much less). Do this five months before starting your fraud so the data is in the system.

The state will want to interact with these 100 ACME employees when the fraud starts. For this, the fraud will require addresses for the DOL communication and for the state to mail the debit cards. In order to thwart investigators, do not use an address that ties back to anyone tied to the fraud. Thus, the next step is to open up 100 mailboxes at a company that provides mailbox services. What is a mailbox service company? This is a company that houses a large number of P.O. boxes where anyone can rent a box. That company will give you an address that looks like a real address.

They are especially useful for businesses that want to have a professional presence, when, in reality, they're just a box. There are a number of companies that provide this service and it is important to spread the 100 mailboxes over a number of places (at least 10). The mailbox service will provide a fictitious address for the stolen identity to appear to live and the address is believable. This has a cost of around $40 each per month and this scam will last 6 months. Since this fraud will take five months to start, only one-quarter payment will suffice. 100 x 40 x 6 equals $36,000 but the fraud money will be pouring in by the beginning so the initial outlay before payments start is only about $1,000.

Our total outlay so far is $100 to the Secretary of State, $1,000 for mailbox services, and $10,000 for ACME to pay unemployment benefits, which equals $11,100. Now, let the fraud begin.

ACME shuts its non-existent doors and goes bankrupt. As a consequence, the 100 false employees begin to request unemployment benefits. The requests are made online through the state's web portal.

No one from the state is verifying the identity since registration is now online. You simply submit the request online. What will the DOL do with this request? It takes the requesting identity information and verifies that this person is in the system to determine his or her level of benefits. This is where that self-reported employment data from ACME will come in handy. The 100 fictitious identities that were pre-seeded into the DOL will be exactly what the incoming online request will be checked against. Essentially, one lie will be used to verify the other lie. To the DOL that equals the truth. This is the joy of self-reported data: because government agencies never seem to question where their data is coming from, and if anyone verified the source or not, it's really easy to fool them.

Let's finish up this fraud. The DOL will reach out to ACME to find out if this person did lose their job and other questions. Do not respond. Remember, ACME has gone bankrupt and thus the phone has been turned off, and the mail won't get delivered. The DOL knows this is what happens to bankrupt companies and will begin paying. The average unemployment benefit is around $300 a week and lasts for 26 weeks. Add up the total payments for the 100, 100 x $300 x 26 equals $780,000. Subtract expenses and this fraud is worth over $750,000. Unfortunately for this state, these same 100 stolen identities are going to go ask for tax refunds and food stamps.

CHAPTER THREE

Benefits Gone Astray, And How The Government Deconstructed Our Security

Ask any American, and they'll all tell you how incredibly efficient, streamlined and bullshit-free the government is. Ah, to dream sweet dreams. The sad reality is that when it comes to fraud, the U.S. government provides a virtual breeding ground for budding fraudsters. First, as more Americans receive government benefits, the opportunities for fraud multiply. Government agencies, meanwhile, are making it exceptionally easy for fraudsters to obtain the information they need, by moving many of their interactions online. Did you know that the federal government is not required to report a data breach, even though the state government and other commercial entities are? Why the hell are they so special? Unfortunately, due to large-scale errors, internal fraud, and a lack of giving-a-damn, our government is helping the fraud business boom.

BAD BENEFITS

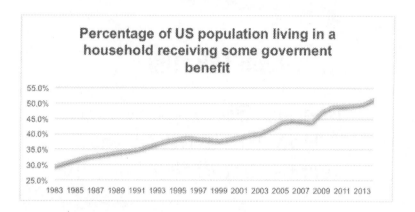

Figure 6: Americans on benefits from 1983-2013[31]

In 2013, about 51 percent of Americans lived in a household where at least one member received a direct government benefit. Many of these households included retirees. Twenty-seven percent were affiliated with a poverty program. We can't and won't get into a debate here over who deserves government benefits or not, over how much individuals receive, and what the words "need" and "help" entail, but one undeniable fact is that because of government fraud, there are most definitely payments going to individuals who do not qualify for the benefits they receive.

According to testimony at a congressional hearing, the United States is making roughly $100 billion in improper payments every year due to a combination of fraud, clerical errors, and insufficient IRS enforcement. The overpayments occur at several agencies, and include tax credits to families that didn't qualify, unemployment benefits to people who had jobs, and medical payments for possibly unnecessary treatments. Identity fraud, in many instances, lies at the basis of improper payments. If a filer applies online, using a

---

[31] Data compiled from multiple GAO reports and Fraud of the Day articles.

fraudulent identity, that certainly counts as an improper payment. In 2013, federal agencies made $97 billion in overpayments, according to agency estimates, while underpayments totaled only $9 billion. $97 billion! And according to congressional investigators, the figures could be even higher.

Each year, federal agencies are required to estimate the amount of improper payments they issue. That includes overpayments, underpayments, payments to the wrong recipient and payments that were made *without proper documentation*. The exact amount of taxpayer money that is wasted through improper payments is unknown, but according to the testimony, the federal government estimates that it is more than half a trillion dollars over the past five years. Some improper payments are the result of fraud, while others are unintentional, caused by clerical "fat-finger" style errors, or mistakes in awarding benefits without proper verification. The largest sources of improper payments are government health care programs, according to agency estimates. Medicare's various health insurance programs for older Americans accounted for $50 billion in improper payments in the 2013 budget year, more than any other program. Here are other programs with a bad history of improper payments:

- **The earned income tax credit: provides payments to the working poor in the form of tax refunds.** Last year, improper payments totaled $14.5 billion. That's 24 percent of all payments under the program. The EITC, one of the largest anti-poverty programs in the U.S.: provided $60.3 billion in payments last year. Eligibility depends on income and family size, making it complicated to apply for the credit — and difficult to control.

- **Medicaid, the government health care program for the poor.** Last year, improper payments totaled $14.4 billion.

- **Unemployment insurance, a joint federal-state program that provides temporary benefits to laid-off workers.** Amount of improper payments last year: $6.2 billion, or 9 percent of all payments. The Labor Department said most overpayments went to people who continued to get benefits after returning to work, or who didn't meet state requirements to look for work while they were unemployed. Others were ineligible for benefits because they voluntarily quit their jobs or were fired.

- **Supplemental Security Income, a disability program for the poor run by the Social Security Administration.** Amount of improper payments: $4.3 billion, or 8 percent of all payments.

Governments trust that the "identities" they see are being accurately presented at the point in time of reporting. Kimberly Little, a senior director of Market Planning at LexisNexis, reminds us that, "Identities are the "people" that government agencies serve – often to enroll in a government program or to receive a government benefit. Federal, state and local government agencies correspond with identities, revenue departments send tax refunds to identities, health care agencies reimburse identities for medical payments and labor departments pay unemployment compensation to identities." To our government, our identities are the only reflections of their constituents that they can see. Because of the flexibility, changeability, and elasticity of identities, too often the government makes an incorrect pairing of an actual person and a fraudulent identity. Governments rely upon rules-based filters and limited, poorly linked data sources to validate identities. Or, too often, they do no validation at all, merely taking the information they are given at face value.

In this chapter, we have highlighted a few agencies and government programs that we think governments should focus on, either because of their importance for giving assistance, or the potential dangers they pose due to easy fraudability and enablement.

EASY PICKINGS: SNAP BENEFITS

Chapter Jackson, a satirist singer, sheds some light on how easy it is to get free benefits, with her YouTube music video, "It's Free, Swipe Yo EBT," in which she calls out a culture that encourages women to have babies so they can help men claim more benefits: "You've got me to get it: Free housing, free day care, free clothes."

What are EBT cards? These are the government's way of delivering Supplemental Nutrition Assistance Program benefits, also known as food stamps. EBT cards are accepted almost everywhere: Small tags on food in grocery stores and convenience stores, hand-written signs on construction paper taped up in gas station and liquor windows tell you where you can use an EBT card.

The economic downturn and consequent loss of jobs have guaranteed a larger portion of Americans going on SNAP benefits. But while the number of food stamp recipients has significantly increased (now up to a total of 45 million, or one in every seven Americans.), the percentage of cases investigated for fraud *has not increased or even remained constant.*[32]

Just as with other agencies, we have no way of exactly how much money is lost to fraudsters. One thing we are certain of: Inefficiency in the food stamp program spending is costing taxpayers billions. Of the $64.7 billion spent on the program last year (a record high that is only slated to increase), an overall $2.5 billion was spent on improper food stamp payments.[33]

Yet, while we can estimate how much is lost to fraud, no state that we have found has a good way of tracking who the fraudsters are.

Take the situation in Iowa. Wendy Dishman, an administrator

[32] Reagan, 2011
[33] Reagan, 2011

of the Investigative Division of the Iowa Department of Inspections and Appeals agrees with the report, stating that the data they collect has a lot of inconsistencies. Apparently, the Food Nutrition Services, which runs SNAP, provided Iowa Watchdog, an investigative news site, with a statement boasting about its success in reducing the percentage of people illegally selling their SNAP benefits.

FNS claims that number has dropped from 4 percent of recipients to 1.3 percent during the past fifteen years. Dishman, however, knows better, "Everybody wonders where the hell they came up with it," she told Watchdog laughingly. "Nobody can explain how they came up with that figure, because what we see is certainly more than that." When Watchdog asked Dishman how common benefit selling — or trafficking, as it is known — is in Iowa, she echoed what we have heard through countless interviews: "Do we think it's increased? Absolutely. But can we prove it? We can't prove it because we don't have the manpower to do it," she said.[34] Wendy Dishman is one of the few government officials who seem to really *get* it, that no, we don't know exactly how much is happening, but we know that it's a lot more than we think it is.

Despite the fact that the number of SNAP recipients in Iowa[35] grew from 295,106 in 2009 to 420,344 in 2013, there's been no increase in federal funding for the Department of Investigations and Appeals to investigate fraud. Seeing as there's little-to-no hope on the funding front, FNS has been trying to utilize technology to help on the front lines of food stamp fraud. The problem? They're using technology that's over 12 years old. As we've learned, fraudsters are tricky little devils. They're hacking into anti-fraud systems within weeks of them being implemented.

Although the technology has been used for several years, Dishman said, "We've received one, maybe two referrals from it."

---

[34] Paul Brennan, "Feds have no idea the extent of SNAP fraud, says Iowa official," *www.Watchdog.Org/169/snap-fraud-iowa/* September 11th, 2014
[35] Food and Nutrition Service, "Average Monthly Participation," 2014

One, maybe two?! Thank God it's free. Dishman, however, is attempting to prevent fraud before it can happen by actually investigating fishy-looking claims. Novel idea. In 2013, DIA investigated 1,277 applicants for SNAP benefits and found incorrect information had been submitted in 899 cases.[36] That would be a little over *70 percent.*

SNAP benefits earns its place as one of our highlighted 'Agencies at Risk' not only because of how important it is that the correct people receive their benefits—and by that, we mean people who need help feeding their families and not fraudsters—but also because of the extreme lack of effort on a wide-scale to help crack down on the problem. We applaud people like Wendy Dishman who are trying to make a difference, despite the fact that the system is working against them.

A VULNERABLE TARGET: DEATH MASTER FILE

The Death Master File (DMF) is a large-scale database that the Social Security Administration owns and administers. It categorizes all the reported (key word being reported here) deaths and the Social Security numbers associated with the people who have died.

Until quite recently, the Death Master File was accessible through ancestry sites, immediately after someone died. Thankfully, ancestry sites and the Social Security Administration have wised up a bit, and now those records are available after three years. While this is a slightly better solution, it's still a gold mine for fraudsters looking for information. As we discussed earlier, one of the major problems with government agencies, from DMVs to Food Stamp offices, is that they are not fully utilizing the Social Security Administration records—due in part to the lack of funding. Even if a fraudster picks up an old Social Security number from the Death Master File, chances are pretty good that it will not be verified by anyone at a

---

[36] Food and Nutrition Service, "State Activity Report," 2014

benefits-giving agency—especially if it's seen to match up with the name they provide.

So we've got a zombie problem. People that have recently died are not being properly reported so they never show up on the DMF. Alternatively, people who have been dead for a long time are magically coming back to life, filing tax returns, getting government benefits, and occasionally, paying their bills. These zombies are digging themselves out of the grave, and are getting away with it for one major reason. Just as fewer and fewer agencies are using the Social Security Administration Social Security number database, so too are they not utilizing the Death Master File. The fraudsters are dipping into government databases like they're scooping out ice cream. The government, meanwhile, verifies few of the applications they receive for benefits.

WHEN NOBODY'S LOOKING: THE IRS

The Internal Revenue Service has been experiencing serious budget cuts, which forces this government agency to juggle way too many responsibilities. The IRS is doing too much, without the ample manpower and funding to support it. Since 2010 the agency's funding has dropped, even though its workload has been expanding. With reduced funding comes reduced services and security, so bad things will begin to happen such as the recent IRS data breach that exposed 334,000 transcript accounts. The IRS then paid out $50 million before they realized they had been had. The criminals got $50 million and a wealth of information after beating the Equifax identity quiz built into the IRS process that protected these transcripts. Not only have we lost the $50 million, but also now the IRS has to deal with thousands of additional fake returns which requires additional personnel and costs. In total the IRS has hired 3,000 phone people just to handle the refund fraud problem.

Last year, the Service examined just one out of every 104 filed returns. Imagine all the potential fraud! Trust us, you're not the only one who is. The individual audit rate for 2014 is expected to drop to 0.80 percent, leaving a mass of unchecked, potentially fraudulent returns unverified, and costing taxpayers potential billions. The IRS recently admitted to Treasury inspectors that it is only able to audit 4 percent of ex-spouses who failed to report alimony that the payer deducted. Meanwhile, a major enforcement initiative, an electronic review program to help find fraudulent returns, has been put on hold.

The money dwindles even further when you realize that as experienced examiners retire, younger, inexperienced examiners are taking their place. More loopholes! It's harder for rookies to get up to speed on complex tax issues such as foreign business activities and multiple pass-through entities. The agency has also had to cut back significantly on its services to taxpayers. Trying to call the IRS? Have you brought along food and water provisions for about a week?

And there's no help coming from taxpayers themselves. In many cases, fraudsters will use identities of individuals who can't stand up for themselves or check in on their identity files. It's not uncommon for children, the elderly, and even the deceased to have their identities stolen and used to file fraudulent tax returns. One fraudster submitted 352 false tax returns in an attempt to make over $800,000 in refunds.[37] He managed to deposit the refunds into several different bank accounts, using the exact methods that we have described here.

The agency no longer answers any tax law questions from taxpayers, making accidental fraudsters out of confused citizens trying to navigate the forms that are well nigh impossible to decipher. Last year, the IRS responded in a timely fashion to fewer than half of taxpayers who protested adjustments. Instead of answering questions, the Service is directing callers to decipher the IRS publications or find the answer on their website. Unless you have a PhD in English, accounting, economics, and sheer patience, you will never find what

---

[37] Office, 2014

you're looking for. They also no longer offer free walk-in tax preparation assistance at its offices. In this case, money begets money. The IRS's 2015 budget is nearly $13 billion and we know that the "admitted" losses due to tax refund fraud is $5.2 billion and the EITC is $14.5 billion. If we give the IRS an additional $1 billion and they stopped just half of the fraud listed above, we would save $10 billion. Not a bad ROI, but the IRS would also have to show a sense of urgency, else the funding would be removed. The IRS needs more funding if it's going to be able to get a better handle on tax fraud. The only real loser here is the U.S. taxpayer, so lets fix this now!

OPEN DOOR TO FRAUD: PUBLIC HOUSING

For this specific fraud, we reached out to John Pomer, from the Everett Massachusetts Housing Authority, to shed some light on some of the problems he and his organization face. The Housing and Urban Development's (HUD) mission is to create strong, sustainable, inclusive communities and quality, affordable homes for people who are physically or financially challenged in ways that make it difficult for them to find or afford housing. HUD's annual budget is $46.6 billion. With a large budget that has to go toward rentals, home sales, mortgages, vouchers, millions of participants, and thousands of employees and landlords, we can begin to understand just how complex HUD's program is. As is a common trend in the fraud game, the more complex (multiple moving parts, lots of employees, different funds) an agency or system is, the easier it is to defraud them. In this way, HUD becomes an ideal target for deception and fraud.

Unfortunately, it's fairly easy to defraud HUD. How? You simply have to lie. As we've seen with many state systems, a lot of agencies will not check to verify your self-reported income. A more complicated, but also more lucrative fraud, would be to steal several identities and try and qualify them for housing. Once those identities are qualified, and we receive some keys, we can rent the units out to people who are under the impression that they are simply regularly rented apartments, and pocket the difference. How would we defraud HUD and its' various programs? Let's list a few methods.

1. One of the easiest and most-frequently performed methods is false representation by the applicant on the application. Usually this deception involves the misrepresentation of personal income or the family composition, such as lying about an undeclared spouse or significant other who also lives in the house and has an income that is not declared.

2. Landlords that are paid by HUD can also defraud HUD by claiming false tenant occupancy.

3. HUD landlords continue to collect the monthly HUD payment from their deceased tenants. Deeply disrespectful, and highly lucrative.

4. Public Housing employees allow friends and or relatives access to housing without application or approval.

5. Employees provide vouchers to friends or family in exchange for kickbacks. They also enable the creation of fictitious landlords and tenants.

6. Tenants qualify for a unit and then sublet it and keep the cash difference.

There is both state-regulated housing that is backed by federal funds, and there is also direct federal housing. State efforts to find and resolve fraud does not extend to federal housing. Often, small, localized governments make stronger attempts at reducing fraud within their own systems, because it impacts them directly. In the case of the Worcester Housing Authority in western Massachusetts, their experts understand that abuse within their agency results in a significant loss, because all fraud funds recovered end up reducing the federal subsidy received by the WHA on a dollar-for-dollar basis.[38]

Simply put, if the WHA recovers $100 of fraud committed by someone living in federally subsidized housing, the federal subsidy to the WHA is reduced by $100. Adding in costs to investigate fraud, and it all ends the same way, with the WHA losing money. Federal housing makes up roughly 83 percent of WHA's total housing. Over the last five years, the Worcester Housing Authority has identified nearly $1.6 million in fraud. The housing-related frauds run the gamut from residents reporting false income to landlords lying about who was renting out their units and for how long. Raymond V. Mariano, the WHA Executive Director, understands that the total number of fraudulent claims discovered is significant. WHA receives roughly $50 million a year in taxpayer support from both state and federal sources. What's more is that about 10,000 people live in the city's public housing and another 12,000 live in leased housing.

Unlike with federal-level fraud, the smaller governments feel the bleed caused by identity fraud much faster, and have a bigger incentive to do something about it. As Mariano said, "There is no incentive to recover and prosecute fraud discovered in the federal public housing." Some examples that have come out of the Worcester housing problem, that are likely replicated in the federal program:

- A woman did not report her husband was living with her in her WHA leased apartment. She also failed to report his

[38] *Telegram.com,* "Report finds $1.6M in Tenant Fraud at Worcester Housing Authority," 2013

income, putting over $30,000 in fraudulent assistance in her pocket.

- One landlord reported a veteran was living in his WHA leased apartment, but the veteran never actually moved in. The landlord never reported it and started receiving monthly WHA money.

7. A resident living in one of the elderly communities owned a BMW. WHA investigated and found the resident was not reporting his true income.

THE MOST DANGEROUS LOOPHOLES: DMVS

Not all government agencies are created equal, just as not all are as vulnerable to fraud. Department of Motor Vehicle fraud happens within every state's DMV. DMV fraud is not only fairly lucrative due to the wide-ranging prices and mass demand of identifications, but it is also a key point of enablement—allowing fraudsters to get away with, well, in all honesty, murder. DMV fraud is a critical building block to enabling identity theft.

So why is the DMV so frequently targeted and so easy to exploit? When an opportunity to simply print a few extra licenses for serious money comes along, why wouldn't an employee jump at it? Aside from an individual's well-to-poorly developed moral compass, there's not much standing in the way. Many 'internal threat' employees do not understand just how extensive their reach is. It's difficult to imagine the one license you illegally make could have such a strong impact. Once that license leaves an employee's hands, it could go on to cause some serious damage, whether they intended for it to or not.

Another reason that DMVs make an easy target is that it's fairly easy to fake the documentation needed to obtain a license. In September, 2012, the Government Accountability Office published an outstanding document about driver's license security and how the federal government needs to step up to address the problems and vulnerabilities within their own agencies. The premise of the report was to spread awareness about how problematic license availability is, and how it can enable criminals to commit crimes from identity theft to acts of terrorism. GAO investigators were able to use counterfeit out-of-state drivers' licenses and birth certificates to fraudulently obtain real licenses in three states. Yes, you understood correctly. GAO investigators managed to get licenses using counterfeit documents.

And finally, DMVs, like other state agencies, do not share information. Most citizens appreciate this perceived respect for privacy, but many do not understand its larger implications. Take, for instance, the story of a friend of ours who moved from Massachusetts to an adjoining state in 2012. He turned in his old license, and received the new one from the new state. About a year later, he received a reminder to renew the old Massachusetts license. Massachusetts was completely unaware that he had moved, even though he surrendered the old license. Stranger yet is the fact that Massachusetts mailed the reminder to the new address *in the adjoining state*.

Figure 7: The notice he received to renew his license in the state he no longer lived in.

This individual asked the Department of Motor Vehicles that sent out the reminder why their agency would solicit a renewal knowing the citizen had moved out of state? Their initial reason was that the old state does not receive notification that the identification has been surrendered, as it's turned into the DMV in the new state. Apparently, states do not cooperatively reconcile surrendered licenses, thus leaving a big black hole of potentially valid licenses.

The other big problem with this is that the DMV mailed the renewal reminder to him in ANOTHER state. Shouldn't this be a big red flag? It's not. Thanks to National Change of Address (NCOA) from the US Postal Service, it looks like the mailing just gets the latest address and is shipped off. Therefore, people can just go online and order a new license from their old state of residence, and since it is still listed as "active", they can get a copy after they have turned one in. Imagine the fun a fraudster has with this loophole.

In another instance, the passing of a man's mother, he needed to look into selling her old car. The car was sitting in his driveway without a title, so, obviously, he needed a replacement title to be able to sell the vehicle. The state in which the woman lived gave a huge amount of paperwork required for them to issue a replacement title for a vehicle belonging to a deceased individual. After finding out that the man's state does not issue some of the required documents requested by her state, he became a little frustrated.

He decided to fill out the paperwork as if she were alive, but have the executor of the estate sign the document. Knowing that they would mail the new title to her old address, despite her being deceased almost a year, the man wasn't sure that the mail would be forwarded to the executor at his address. Sure enough, three weeks later, the new title arrived. Thanks to NCOA forwarding DMV documents, and the DMV not checking to see if the woman was deceased, the man was able to obtain a new title with the legitimate owner being deceased.

All of these problems cited above, contribute to providing

numerous loopholes for fraudsters to exploit. Is this a big issue? Yes. Especially when considering 2.5 percent of the population moves between states each year. That's 7.8 million people annually that the states lose track of, who could potentially file for additional driver's licenses.

Traditionally, verifying license applicants' identities and keeping fraud to a minimum was the role of the state. After the terrorist attacks of September 11, however, the federal government became increasingly concerned about how driver's licenses are issued and the security surrounding the process, as evidenced by the passage of the REAL ID Act of 2005. The Act does not mandate that states comply with the measures, but establishes specific procedures states must follow when issuing drivers' licenses in order for those licenses to be accepted by federal agencies for "official purposes," including, but not limited to, boarding commercial aircraft, entering federal buildings, and entering nuclear power plants. You've heard of the Pirate Code? It's more about guidelines than actual rules, allowing pirates to do pretty much what they want. The states have been treating the REAL ID Act like a Pirate Code. As of July 2012, 17 states had enacted laws expressly opposing implementation or prohibiting the relevant state agencies from complying with the REAL ID Act.

The REAL ID Act sets minimum standards for several aspects of the license and identification card issuance process. If the standards were being implemented, they would help a lot. State driver licensing agencies use a combination of different techniques to verify the identity of license applicants and prevent fraud. These various procedures are used together to detect license fraud and no single technique is sufficient, according to officials at several licensing agencies. In the area of identity verification, the Act establishes the following requirements, among others, for states seeking compliance:

1. 1. **Documentation**: States must require license applicants to provide documentation of their name, date of birth, Social

Security number, address of principal residence, and lawful status in the United States.

2. **Verification**: Requires states to verify with the issuing agency the issuance, validity, and completeness of the documents presented as proof of name, date of birth, Social Security number (or verify the applicant's ineligibility for a Social Security number), address, and lawful status, with specific requirements to confirm Social Security numbers with the Social Security Administration and verify lawful status of non-citizens through an electronic Department of Homeland Security system.

3. **Image capture**: Requires states to capture and store digital images of all documents presented by license applicants to establish identity, such as passports and birth certificates, and capture the facial images of all applicants.

4. **Renewals**: Requires states to establish an effective procedure for confirming or verifying the information provided by individuals seeking to renew their licenses.

5. **One driver, one license**: Requires states to refuse to issue a license to an applicant who already holds a license from another state, without confirming that this other license has been or is in the process of being terminated.

6. **Staff training**: Establish training programs on recognizing fraudulent documents for appropriate employees involved in issuing licenses.

The REAL ID Act also specifies the information that must be displayed on licenses and requires that licenses include security features designed to prevent counterfeiting. Also, it requires states to ensure the physical security of the locations where licenses are made and requires employees who work in the manufacturing of licenses to be subject to an appropriate security clearance process.

Most states are also using Systematic Alien Verification for Entitlements (SAVE), another REAL ID Act requirement, but several still remain noncompliant, thus opening up their own agencies and American citizens to potential identity fraud. Many states that were interviewed that were not using SAVE blamed technological challenges, like problems with providing front-counter staff in local issuance branches with routine access to the system.

Officials in half of the states interviewed that were using SAVE said they were concerned about the verification rate they obtained. When states submit data from non-citizens' lawful status documents, the system searches a variety of Department of Homeland Security databases in an effort to verify the information. If data is not verified on the first attempt, the state can check a second and third time, which can rack up costs for the state (a.k.a., for you). Several states do not verify Social Security numbers through an on-line verification system when people renew their licenses. Apparently, state officials don't think it's necessary to take this step because these Social Security numbers were already verified at the time of initial license application. The problem here is obvious: If the person who applied for the license in the first place was a fraudster, the fake ID can be issued in perpetuity. Oh well, you win some, you lose some. At least, that seems to be the state's attitude.

This all sounds good, but when you look at the stats it's not impressive. As of July 2015 of the fifty states and six U.S. territories, here is the overall adoption rate of the 2005 Real-ID program. Twenty-three states/territories comply, twenty-eight are asking for another extension (they have had five). Five are remaining non-compliant. Homeland Security originally had May 2008 as the original deadline. This has been pushed back to December of 2009, March 2011,

January 2013, and now it stands at December 2016. If Homeland Security had a backbone and stopped citizens from getting on planes via TSA, which they run, this would be solved in a few months.

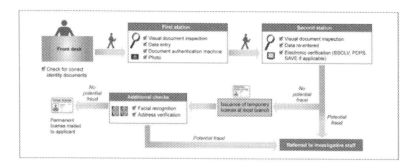

Figure 8: Identity verification process in one state, as shown in a 2012 GAO report, compiled from interviews conducted with state officials.

The word "non-compliant" sounds serious. Darth Vader would threaten the free world with something like this: "If you remain non-compliant, the consequences will be dire." In this republic, however, remaining non-compliant could actually cause significant harm to our national security. Being able to really know who is boarding an airplane, who is driving a car and crossing borders, heck, who is buying a six-pack at the corner store, is really important, because if we don't know who's doing it, the consequences could actually be dire.

WHY ARE THERE SO MANY LOOPHOLES?

Everybody knows that you're more likely to get a speeding ticket towards the end of the month. Police officers have a quota to fill on speeding tickets every month, and so the last few days they're out in heavy patrol, trying to fill those numbers. The quotas are in place because the success of the system is measured by the number of tickets they give away. What most people don't know, however, is that government benefit agencies work in a similar fashion. A certain benefit program's success is measured on how many benefits they give out and how much money they give away. This one factor has so many implications. It means that government benefit programs would rather just give away money if they have a question about verification rather than be wrong. It's simply bad press. Many government officials have the same kind of mindset when it comes to tightening verification policies on benefits.

Another of the underlying conditions contributing to government fraud is what our team has coined **Boundary Blindness**. Boundary Blindness is the lack of information regarding a claimant due to a border or a government program boundary. Border boundaries are state or county lines. The state or county has a limited view of information outside its own borders. Program boundaries refer to stove-piped programs that cannot or do not share information with other programs. For example, if Vermont and Connecticut are both paying unemployment to Patty Jones due to the lack of information sharing, it's an issue of state-level blindness. This issue is very common, and becoming more so.

One reason states don't share information, often, is due to the risk incurred when data is lost or stolen. If Missouri lends Wyoming driver's license information, and Wyoming's system is hacked, Missouri ends up being responsible to their citizens whose information was exposed.

Take the man from Cambridge, Massachusetts, who used the identity of an out-of-state man to steal tens of thousands of dollars in government benefits. The fraudster used the name of a man with a similar name that lived in a different state, and forged a birth certificate to apply for benefits. Since 2005, he has received at least $65,000 in state benefits including MassHealth, Supplemental Nutrition Assistance Program, and Emergency Aid for the Elderly, Disabled and Children. The man, who claimed to be financially unable to make ends meet, could not apply for the benefits himself because he had outstanding warrants for his arrest for unrelated crimes, including larceny and operating a motor vehicle with a suspended license. Investigators said that the man received a replacement Social

Security card in his victim's name in 1994, a Massachusetts driver's license in the victim's name in 1996, and a Massachusetts identity card in the victim's name in 2008.[39]

This is not just an example of Boundary Blindness (had Massachusetts been able to look across state lines, they would have seen that the identity being used by the fraudster belonged to someone who did not actually live in Massachusetts), but also an example of enablement. Boundary Blindness allowed a wanted criminal to live freely off of the identity of another person. Due to the lack of access to data across state lines, there's no way to verify self-reported information given to agencies by their citizens, therefore the information is usually assumed true and the claim is paid. Some government programs that are directly impacted by Boundary Blindness are as follows:

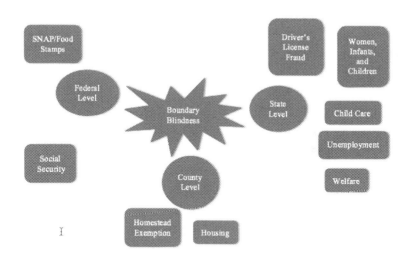

Figure 9: Boundary Blindness and its widespread effects on government benefit programs

---

[39] Boston Globe, "Cambridge man charged with stealing ID in benefits scam," 2012.

Often, states do not have the information that citizens seem to think they do. Boundary Blindness is a huge enabler to identity fraud. Remember that *18 of the 19 terrorists involved in the 9/11 attacks held over 30 valid driver's licenses and identification cards issued by five states.* The reason that the terrorists had obtained so many state identifications was to escape detection by airport security systems that use passport data to check foreign visitors against federal watch lists. Because the state DMVs are not able to see across state boundary lines, they were unable to know that the terrorists had already obtained driver's licenses from other states. Boundary Blindness isn't just a state-level issue. The federal government is bleeding from it as well.

This lack of information sharing can have devastating effects. One 53-year-old man, a rapist who eluded police for more than three decades, managed to escape arrest by fleeing to Maine from Massachusetts after his 1979 convictions. He lived as a free man under his brother's identity without being detected. He married, had two children, and *obtained and repeatedly renewed a Maine driver's license,* all while Massachusetts continued to list him as one of its most wanted fugitives. If Maine and Massachusetts had been sharing information, police in Maine could have known to question the man's brother. Or, if digital images were available across state lines, an image might have made the capture too. But it took police thirty-four years to find this man after a tip from a family member after a family dispute. All because their internal state systems could not, and would not, share information with other state systems.

One more example from the annals of boundary blindness, this time between agencies. In 2009 the Internal Revenue Service processed and paid out $12.1 million in fraudulent tax refund claims submitted using the stolen names and Social Security numbers of 5,108 dead people. The IRS never bothered to check with the Social Security Administration's Death Master File. And get this. The claims were all filed under the ID number assigned to just one tax preparer -- which should have been another tip-off. And finally, the IRS doesn't share information about the fraud it finds with the state. So a fraudster could well take these same stolen identities and use them to fraud the states. IRS and states do have a working relationship, but do not share identities.

Our response: If agencies would work together, this fraud could have been stopped at multiple points in the system.

NON-VERIFICATION

In 2011, IRS Inspector General J. Russell George told the United States House Ways and Means Committee that the IRS requires no documentation to prove eligibility for the education credit. The report found, in part, that in 2010, 1.7 million tax filers received $2.6 billion in education credits with no supporting documentation in IRS files that they attended school. The sheer lack of verification in government agencies is appalling.

One of the major verification issues with the Affordable Care Act, passed in 2010, is the difficulty in verifying enrollees. Many applicants are not eligible for coverage, and the people in charge are having a difficult time telling the legitimate from the fraudsters. Nearly 1.3 million Affordable Care Act enrollees, or about 16 percent of the overall total, cannot be verified for legal status in the United States for various reasons, according to the Office of the Inspector General. According to the figures, over one million "inconsistencies"— this is a politically correct way of implying missing or fraudulent data—found on Affordable Care Act applications involved issues of citizenship, national status, or lawful presence in the United States, meaning applicants did not or could not verify this information. This lack of verification in the healthcare sector points to a much bigger problem overall—what else are we missing?

Well let's look at something simple like non-verification of addresses. The Social Security Administration relies heavily on the post office's National Change of Address (NCOA) database to provide the latest address information for a beneficiary. With the simple change of address form from the post office, a criminal can easily have someone else's mail diverted to an address that he or she controls allowing them to obtain information to perpetrate a fraud. Assuming that was the case, read the letter pictured here from the Social Security Administration.

Social Security Administration
Retirement, Survivors and Disability Insurance
Important Information

Date: September 29, 2014
Claim Number: ████████████

ᵐᵘᵖᵖᵖ᛫ᵈᵘᴵᴵ

We are writing about your mailing address. The United States Postal Service has told us that they have a mailing address for you that is different from the mailing address on our records.

What You Need To Do

The mailing address the Post Office gave us is shown above. If you told us about this new address within the last 45 days, you can ignore this letter and you do not need to contact us.

If you did not tell us about this address, and the address is correct, **you do not need to contact us.** We will change your mailing address on our records in about 30 days from the date of this letter.

If you do not want us to use this address, or the address is not correct, please call us at the number shown below.

If You Have Questions

If you have any questions, you may call us toll-free at 1-800-772-1213, or call your local Social Security office at 866-964-4324. We can answer most questions over the phone. You can also write or visit any Social Security office. The office that serves your area is located at:

███████████ 0-4091

PLEASE DO NOT WRITE TO THE RETURN ADDRESS SHOWN ON THE ENVELOPE. If you do call or visit an office, please have this letter with you. It will help us answer your questions.

████████   *Social Security Administration*

Figure 10: A Social Security Administration form requesting a change of address

In this case, the SSA has blindly taken the Post office's change of address information as correct. The SSA has not done any third party address verification, therefore allowing the fraudster to simply submit a change of address under a retirees name, and all of the retiree's SSA correspondence will automatically be diverted to the fraudsters address. Have you ever gone to the post office and done a change of address? Fill out a 5x7 card and hand it to the postal worker, no ID is needed.

It has become too easy to lie to our government, and to receive compensation for doing so. If anything is going to change, it won't come from the fraudsters' end. It will come in the form of the government stepping up, blocking out potential criminals, and punishing the fraudsters.

We've discussed the problems of government agencies migrating to the web without implementing verification and authentication systems for those applying on-line, but another huge problem is that agencies have been cut to the bone. Reduced headcount and increased workload force work to be passed through without review. Employees therefore cannot mitigate threats to the agency such as hackers, and fraudsters. Because of these forced budget cuts, many agencies are hesitant to pay for verification or authentication services or access. Department of Motor Vehicles also have to pay verification fees. DMVs Social Security number verification costs five cents per individual look-up, or ¼ of a penny for batch lookups.[40] Some DMVs will not pay and thus do not check the authenticity of Social Security numbers.

Other internal government employee issues include management not wanting to appear inefficient or slow, and eliminating checks and verification as a result. One high-level government executive we spoke with during one of our information sessions worked in a state department of revenue. He told us that he didn't want to learn any new systems to teach to his employees, as he was soon retiring.

---

[40] United States Government Accountability Office, 2012

It's already a bad excuse, but especially so because he wouldn't be retiring for the next seven years!

Government agencies that have long claimed 1 percent fraud rates are now showing 7-9 percent fraud rates, or more. It's tough to defend yourself when upper management asks some hard questions like, "Have you been doing your job?" The omnipresent attitude that "no one gets fired from government" needs to be overturned, and pronto. Remember the story of the unemployed woman who was issued a debit card for $2.1 million dollars after claiming she made $3 million? (She's the one who bought the used van.) After the dust settled, *three Department of Revenue employees were reprimanded and one was demoted.* That's it. In our current system, there is no accountability for mistakes. That state lost $2.1 million dollars and a couple of people got yelled at? Government agencies need to put structures in place to help motivate their employees to do their jobs correctly, and place stricter punishments upon them for giving the fraudsters a leg up. It's a serious issue when it's easier to get fired from a fast food joint than the Department of Revenue.

How to Fraud 103: Tax Refund Fraud

To successfully pull off a tax refund fraud, we can pick one of two options. There's a simple way to fraud this system, and a more complex method. If we are only going to steal a small amount of money then the simple method is fine. If we are going all in, then we will need to move to the more advanced method below.

What We Need:
1. Some stolen identities (easily obtained from doctors' offices, schools, etc.)

2. A computer with a tax application

3. An Internet connection.

Our first step is to buy some identities online, or we can arrange to steal a few from a place of work or business. Thanks to the numerous breaches at big retailers, the going prices for other people's identities are relatively low. Rather than go dumpster diving or hire someone to pocket some office forms, we can buy roughly 100 identities for under $1,000. Now we need a few laptops with a tax submission application.

Our first big decision will be whether we're going to steal from the IRS or a state. The IRS's limit for tax returns is $10,000 (before a flag is triggered on your file), and most states' is $2,000, so we want to stay below those numbers on our applications to avoid triggering any red flags. We'll file a few tax returns and have the checks sent to a PO box or a neighbor's address, preferably a neighbor that works all day and whose mailbox we have access to. This is the quickest and easiest way to make a few dollars.

Performing a complex tax refund fraud adds a few steps. We'll start with the basic components listed above, but as we shift into high production we need to be aware of a few issues. The IRS and most states are now looking for duplicate IP addresses, to help cut back on the individuals, such as ourselves, who are filing multiple returns. We'll visit a few apartment complexes, fast food joints, and the public library to find open Internet connections. These hotspots will allow us to connect and send the bogus tax forms to the IRS and the states without creating more suspicion.

The IRS's has recently changed the filing date so that W-2 forms and tax returns need to be submitted at the same time, so that they can match. But while the IRS was trying to make their system more cohesive, what it did was make it easier for us to fraud. We can make up a W-2, submit it as "proof" alongside a tax return, and request a hefty sum as a return. Filing false tax returns is still a very simple procedure, and with the right focus, we should be able to file about 50 returns a day.

Now, we need to determine how we would like to get paid. Do we want a physical check, direct deposit or do we want a debit card? There are pros and cons with each of these methods of payment. A physical check requires that we have an actual address to receive it, and be able to show a form of identification and have an account to cash it. With video cameras operating within most banks, the likelihood that we could be identified rises. So let's move on.

Direct deposit is nice since all we have to do is go online and create an account with a stolen identity. We then have the funds deposited electronically, and withdraw them at an ATM. The only catch is that we need to receive the ATM card at the address tied to the identity. But thankfully, with the National Change of Address service we can temporarily have that mail routed to our PO box. Not bad, but not perfect.

Simple and easy is what we're aiming for here, so debit cards are the best way to go. We'll have the card mailed to our PO box, and we're done! With this method, there is no tie from the card to the holder. It's like having cash, but on a piece of plastic!

Though they provide fewer funds per return, the benefit of scamming states is that we can reuse the identities as long as we are submitting in states that the victim does not reside or file in. With the IRS, the victims will likely file with the IRS (unless they're a fraudster like us, or dead), and this will tip them off that their identity has been compromised.

CHAPTER FOUR

The Fraud Of The Future: Healthcare Fraud

Fraudsters are already living in the future. To keep up with them, we need to ask the question: What are the conditions now in government agencies and our society that could change the future, and how might they change things?

Fraudsters are saving identities, stocking up to sell them on the black market, or possibly just waiting until you let your guard down and forget to check on your Social Security file this year. One of the most important aspects of understanding identity fraud is seeing how it will affect the future, and what we can do to try to stop it before it happens.

Perhaps the biggest concern about the future of the fraud is the number of people who will be capable of undertaking it. The technological boom of the 1990s and early 2000s brought widespread Internet access, and a new group of tech-savvy fraudsters. The Internet, smart phones, public Wi-Fi, and social networking sites turned fraud into a new game, and a vastly more accessible one at that. Take, for example, an Austrian boy arrested in 2012 and accused of hacking 259 companies within the span of three months. As Phil Ostwalt, a partner in KPMG Forensic, states, "Cybercrime brings with it a different type of fraudster: a younger, educated person without corporate experience but having learned the business playing with technology early on. This person has the power to do extensive damage to companies."

We pointed out how technology makes your personal information vastly more accessible, and how it weakens government agencies' communication with their customers and constituents. Younger fraudsters are more comfortable with technology, especially the Internet. Millennials, unlike any other generation, have grown up with omni-present technology. Even the oldest Millennials—for the most part—had an awareness of the Internet and its capabilities from a young age. People who are getting interested in technological development are no longer solely people with advanced degrees—they're middle-schoolers with an iPhone and an understanding of how applications are made, but without the judgment of an adult. This comfort and easy understanding of how technology works already gives potential fraudsters in this age range a leg-up on their predecessors. They already understand the language of hacking, and how to hide behind their computer screen.

We also worry about the growing anonymity of the Internet. People online wear a weird Internet mask that lets them say whatever they're thinking without a filter. If you have ever scrolled through the comments section of a YouTube video, you can understand this kind of blind dialogue. Normally, if you were learning to play guitar, and were practicing in an open-air space like a park, no more than a handful of really terrible people would call out your awful playing directly to your face. Yes, they might snicker behind their hands, but the outlandish comparisons of your playing to that of a cat vomiting or squealing car tires would be few and far between.

On the Internet, however, people get to hide behind their screens, and likewise, the people on the other end don't seem as much like flesh and blood humans as they do like a funny video you can respond to with horrifically nasty comments. It seems like a far jump from saying something mean online to stealing someone's identity, but many online identity thieves disassociate numbers and 'identities' with the actual human beings attached to them. This mental severing allows identity thieves to carry less of a mental burden when stealing someone's identity, because to them, they don't seem so much like individuals as they do series of numbers that can help pay their electricity bill.

FRAUD AND SOCIAL MEDIA

On the other hand, fraudsters' lack of self-consciousness could be their undoing. Some fraudsters seem to think that the Internet is the Wild West of the modern world. Some see it as lawless, as a sounding board to brag about criminal activity. What they don't realize is that nobody likes a bragger, and that just like in real life, someone can report you to the authorities—even just by tweeting the local police's twitter account.

In fact, one woman, who was later charged with identity theft, possession of a false government document and forgery, was identified by the New Jersey State Police department, after the police posted a video of incriminating surveillance photographs of her withdrawing money using a fake driver's license. The police department posted the video on their Facebook page—which was then shared over 5,700 times—and the woman was found the same day.[41]

While it is exciting to see criminals apprehended through social media, we also see how attitudes are changing to reflect fraud as an "acceptable crime." Thoughts on accepting and taking advantage of government assistance as a whole are changing as well. The Internet has created a new world for fraudsters to make money, as we've discussed. This world comes complete with a new atmosphere, and new ideas.

Take the story of the woman who called herself the First Lady

---

[41] Nguyen, 2014

of Tax Fraud, claimed to be an income tax fraud pioneer, and taught others how to commit fraud. The Queen, as we affectionately call her, openly bragged on Facebook about her fraudulent endeavors, about taking expensive trips and about having so much money that she forgot about a purse full of cash in her closet. "YES I'M R***** THE QUEEN OF IRS TAX FRAUD," reads one of her more blatant Facebook statuses. "IM' A MILLIONAIRE FOR THE RECORD SO IF U THINK INDICTING ME WILL BE EASY IT WONT I PROMISE U!"

Apparently, The Queen posted a picture of herself wearing an oversized jewel-encrusted pendant spelling out her first name while holding bundles of cash. Despite her atrocious spelling and grammar, The Queen and her boyfriend filed more than 220 fraudulent tax returns claiming $1.9 million in refunds between 2009 and 2012. Most of the refunds were approved by the IRS, which sent out nearly $1.3 million. When the woman was indicted, it was based off the calculation that she had, in total, managed to steal $3.1 million. Later investigations showed that she could have stolen anywhere from $7 million to $20 million.[42]

These numbers are not exactly close, which gives some good insight into just how difficult it is to know how much money is walking out the door in most identity fraud cases. The self-proclaimed Queen was one of the flashiest fraudsters who was operating during Tampa's income tax fraud explosion, and a perfect example of how to get yourself caught. The Queen was no experience-hardened young woman, she was taking what she could get without a second thought, and the IRS was sending her almost $3.1 million—without a second thought.

Facebook has become the number one social networking site on the planet. With over one billion users, it has become common to, instead of asking for someone's email, simply friend them on

---

[42] Silvestrini, 2013

Facebook. What many users do not understand is how vulnerable these social media accounts make them. Many users put their address, phone number, and email address on their account without thinking twice. Ever wished someone a happy birthday? That means that they have their actual birthdate on this site, coupled with their name, and a photo, tagged at their home location, gives potential fraudsters just enough information to start compiling a synthetic identity.

Just how much personal information can be gleaned from someone's Facebook account becomes evident in the indictments of more than 130 police officers, firefighters and other civil servants on charges of defrauding the Social Security system with fake disability claims. Facebook photos of the suspects showed supposedly disabled people riding personal watercraft, teaching karate, deep-sea fishing and pursuing other vigorous activities. Those photos supported other evidence, like wiretapped conversations, that prosecutors gathered in their three-year investigation.[43] Just as in the case with the Tax Fraud Queen, Facebook is viewed by many as a safe place to advertise one's personal (and illegal) accomplishments.

So why is this happening? Aside from the obvious—people who are unaware of the Internet's power to bring criminals to justice— why are people suddenly outing themselves? Perhaps it's because, in some small way, crime has always been cool, and now we have a way to share it. In other ways, though, we see attitudes toward fraud at large changing.

Identity fraud rates are skyrocketing—but is it just because it's easier to do now? If people always had the Internet, would they always have taken advantage of its offerings, or is there a deeper, moral implication? These are questions that we cannot answer, but something that we do know is that identity fraud is a crime of opportunity. Just as with anonymous YouTube comments, it's easier

---

[43] Goel, 2014

to commit a crime against someone that you cannot see and you do not know than to commit a crime against someone who is right in front of you. Stealing someone's wallet is probably far less harmful (forgoing any psychological trauma that could have been caused) to an individual's financial situation than stealing their identity, but far *more* people would be willing to steal an identity online than steal someone's wallet in person. Additionally, identity fraud is becoming more visible. Identity fraud can be seen everywhere these days—and not just in newspaper headlines. We mean everywhere.

FRAUD IN POP CULTURE

Whether art is reflecting life or life is reflecting art, the portrayal of identity fraud in art is booming almost as big as the identity fraud industry itself. We are starting to see it loom large in popular culture. It has seeped into television shows, movies, and celebrity Twitter feeds. There are more depictions than just the story of Frank Abagnale, the world's most exciting fraudster, in *Catch Me If You Can*. The 2013 film *Identity Thief* portrays average businessman Sandy Patterson, a man whose identity was stolen by a woman who called to confirm some personal details. The film shows a hilarious hunt by the original Sandy Patterson to find the fraudulent one, only to eventually tie up in a cute ending with the two becoming close, and learning life lessons from one another.

You may be familiar with the hugely popular Netflix-released television series *Orange is the New Black*, which relates one woman's experience in the American prison system. Actress Selenis Yeyva portrays inmate Gloria Mendoza, a woman who was sentenced for exchanging Food Stamps for money, and then reporting to the government on the goods she didn't actually sell—making a bundle in the process. In this case, Mendoza is sympathetically shown, as having no other options, with an abusive boyfriend, and a failing convenience store in the picture. This portrayal gives a face to some of the people who commit fraud because it seems to them that they have no other choice. Though of course still illegal, these kinds of fraudsters are far more sympathetic than the millionaires who are on welfare.

If we can put a stop to identity fraud, keep the people out of government benefits who do not actually need them or qualify for them, then people like the character of Gloria Mendoza will not have to resort to fraudulent means to support their families. The frequency of identity fraud being portrayed on television and other means has skyrocketed. Shows like *American Greed*, *Scam City*, and *Fraud Squad* are entirely focused on showcasing fraud, either in real or fictional instances. Fraud is on people's minds; it's how these shows, movies, and characters find success in pop culture. So if it's showing up in American cultural expression, shouldn't that be a sign that it's a widespread problem? Just as the plethora of Red Scare films made in the mid 1950's highlighted a growing fear and distrust of Communism, the growing popularity of identity theft and fraud features in popular media should tell us something about what people are afraid of now in the 21st century.

For people who are familiar with the popular television show, *The Real Housewives of New Jersey*, they know that this show has perpetual drama. One thing they may not know, however, is the real life drama that broke out in October 2014. Teresa Giudice, one of the stars on the show, was sentenced to 15 months in prison, and her husband 41 months, on conspiracy and bankruptcy charges.[44] So what does a desperate housewife of New Jersey do when she hears about her sentence? She throws a 'Stays Strong' party at a club. This is no joke, but only a reflection of how attitudes toward punishment and jail time are being perceived in our country and culture. Figures in the limelight have always misbehaved—from Jacobean England up to Bernie Madoff—but the more publicized they become, the more numb we become to it, and the more acceptable it seems.

---

[44] The Associated Press, "Teresa," 2014

Giudice's flippant behavior towards her sentencing throws into her fans' faces the changing attitudes toward fraudulent behavior—and that it's no big deal. These kinds of attitude adjustments, as they are reflected in wide-scale pop culture, show a shifting mindset about the acceptability and ease of perpetrating fraud.

THE NEXT SHOE TO DROP

Where is this all taking us? Where is identity fraud heading, and what kind of preventative measures can we take to safeguard against what is only a rising execution of identity fraud? We can look at the next shoe to drop. One new area of concern: healthcare, which has become a cesspool of fraudulent activity. Medicare/Medicaid currently has a $74 billion annual fraud rate, which is approximately 10 percent of all expenditures. Attitudes toward fraud in general are changing, especially with regard to the Internet. How can we corral these, and other future factors in the identity fraud game, to change how we will handle fraud in the future?

National healthcare is a new and highly complex treasure trove for fraudsters. The size of the budgets for just Medicaid and Medicare alone are large enough that they are often viewed as bottomless, now at over $1 trillion per year. Not only are their budgets enormous, but so are their client pools. One out of six Americans receives Food Stamp benefits; 100 percent of Americans are supposed to have health insurance. With so many more people inculcated with fraudulent notions, and so many more individuals having health care to begin with, the opportunities for fraud to occur only increase. The complexities of national healthcare are owed in part to the number of players involved. There are patients, providers, insurers, and of course state and federal government. Consider the amount of personal information captured and retained on patients, healthcare workers, and the varying technology that is used or could be used to capture and steal that information. It is also vital to understand that because of these technologies' ubiquity, nearly every patient and healthcare worker is able to gain access to them.

The Ponemon Institute performed a study on Patient Privacy and Data Security, which concluded that 90 percent of healthcare organizations in this study had at least one data breach.

Figure 1. Experienced a data breach involving the loss of patient data in the past two years

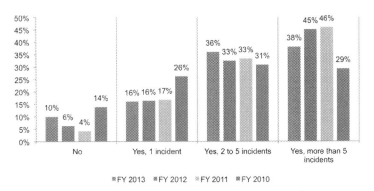

Figure 11: A poll of healthcare organizations that experienced a data breach involving the loss of patient data in the past two years. If you add together the total number of incidents, it shows that 38 percent of healthcare organizations reported more than five incidents.[45]

Medical facilities have developed processes and procedures to keep patient information safe. Trying to safeguard data from individuals with criminal intent while making the information accessible to those that are looking for the data to help the patient becomes an almost impossible task. If it were as simple as keeping those outside the facility from accessing information, it would be easy, but technological advances have made it so there are previously non-existent doors that can be opened. The challenge lies in determining who internally and externally should have access and when. It becomes evident when those internally are careless, make an error, or even

---

[45] Ponemon Institute, 2014

intentionally decide to steal information. Imagine a screen showing patient information or a paper file left open on a desk. If an employee, patient or even a visitor wants to steal that information, he or she just needs to snap a picture and click send. All within a few seconds, private information is captured and transmitted without a trace to an outside location. How many people have access to smart phones, how many of those people carry them everywhere?

As we began to discuss in the previous chapter, the new standard of national healthcare has opened up a lot of doors. Healthcare has become easier to access for some people. But fraudsters are simply leaping at the opportunities and loopholes the Affordable Care act seems to present. Contributing factors include the documentation of unsecure websites and databases and health information exchanges that are vulnerable to insider and outsider threats. As the Ponemon Institute study points out, "while the total number of data breaches has declined slightly over previous years, almost every healthcare organization represented in this research had a data breach."[46]

The volume of information and identities coupled with the complexities of medical systems all increases by an order of magnitude. If the government had problems before, they certainly have bigger ones now. Data breaches can range in expense from $10,000 to more than $1 million. The study estimates that the average cost for the organizations represented is approximately $2 million over a two-year period. Their guess, based off previous studies and this one, is that the potential cost to the healthcare industry could be as much as $5.6 billion every single year.[47]

The study pointed out several issues happening with the healthcare industry on a large-scale that make these companies more vulnerable to identity fraud. Most of these issues are technology-based, as we've seen any kind of large-scale technological advancement allows fraud to seep through the cracks. The Ponemon study points

[46] Ponemon Institute, p. 2, 2014
[47] --, p. 2, --

out that criminal attacks on healthcare organizations have increased 100 percent since 2010, and that insider negligence continues to be a serious part of most major data breaches.[48] Data breaches, especially with regard to sensitive data (patient and employee information, etc.) jumped—striking a frightening chord for healthcare organizations attempting to address the criminal intent behind these kind of breaches.

Among the polled organizations, it appears that employee negligence is considered the biggest security risk.[49] Other concerns included mobile device insecurity and cyber attackers. Similarly to the Department of Motor Vehicles security issues, employee security is a serious concern. Healthcare schemes almost always include an inside person. Human error will always be a factor in fraudulent concerns. However, offering strong incentives to employees to remain loyal to the company, using background check tools, and varying claims handling are all ways in which these kind of breaches, and the ensuing identity fraud, can be kept in check.

The specific technological advancements used by the healthcare industry, and thus abused by fraudsters operating in the healthcare industry, are such every day pieces of equipment that it's frightening to fathom how easy it is to access sensitive information. Eighty-eight percent of healthcare organizations permit employees and medical staff to use their own mobile devices such as smart phones or tablets to connect to their organization's networks or enterprise systems such as email, despite the fact that more than half of organizations are not confident that the personally owned mobile devices are secure.[50] The implications of medical personnel being able to connect to the same network that holds all of a healthcare company's sensitive information on their personal devices are enormous. These

---

[48] --, p. 3, --

[49] --, p. 3, --

[50] --, p. 3, --

companies are essentially holding open the door for potential fraudsters to walk right through.

Hospitals are moving toward a centralized repository model that can be accessed, administered and secured, also known as cloud computing. There are many benefits to this model, but challenges and vulnerabilities also exist. Cloud computing is a wonderful concept until it breaks down. There is no guarantee that the enclosed files are encrypted, and no assurance that even if they are, that hackers cannot access encryption keys to decrypt the data. There is no guarantee that administrators will not make an error leaving the entire cloud vulnerable. 2014 saw several kinds of breaches like this, ranging from private celebrity photo leaks to the Sony breach, which lost not only emails, contracts, personal and financial information of employees and stars, but actual pre-released movies. It happens to someone in the world daily; imagine the damage when it happens in healthcare.

"Cloud computing gives companies and government agencies numerous benefits such as economies of scale and reduced spending on technology infrastructure, but the fact remains that the only true way to guarantee 100 percent data security against Internet based threats is to unplug from the Internet," says Shawn Smolsky, a senior IT solutions architect for Lockheed Martin. There will never be 100% data assurance with all the insider threats and physical access issues, but Smolsky has a point. If we are going to utilize the Internet, cloud computing, and widespread network access, we have to be ready to mitigate the risks and make sure those doors are as securely locked to fraudsters as we can make them.

In addition to allowing personnel to connect to their networks for personal usage, healthcare companies are also really using cloud services. Only one-third of the polled organizations are very confident or confident that information in a public cloud environment is secure. Despite the acknowledged risk, 40 percent of organizations say they use the cloud heavily. The applications or services most used are backup and storage, file-sharing applications, business applications and document sharing and collaboration.[51]

Given the abundant data breaches that have occurred in the healthcare sector, we must begin to consider the wider-reaching implications. As we explained in our opening chapter, data breaches *expose* information; they do not guarantee that information has immediately begun to be used for identity fraud. It does, however, seriously up the odds that that information will be used, sold, or altered in the future. Healthcare fraud looks a lot like government fraud.

Just as with a benefits program, individuals can fraudulently submit information and receive payments. Due to the jump in health care fraud, estimates are that *10 cents of every dollar spent on health care goes toward paying for fraudulent health care claims.*[52] Some of this is fraud that insurance companies pay for, but much of it is fraud aimed at the two large government programs involved in paying for health care: Medicaid, the government health care programs for the poor, and Medicare, the government health care program for the elderly. When either of these agencies are defrauded, it affects the whole system. What the government pays for procedures from surgery to physical therapy sets the standard for non-governmental payers, too.

The opportunities for fraud begin the moment a patient walks into any kind of health-related facility—whether that's a hospital, a chiropractor's waiting room, or a dentist's office. Mostly, schemes come in at place of billing. As soon as money starts getting exchanged, things can start to look a little dicey. An office could bill you for a service not actually rendered, in that it charges Medicare for medical services that were never actually administered or performed (amazing how they can bill for a hysterectomy on a man, and still get paid!). There's also Medicare billing fraud, where maybe a doctor adds a few extra procedures, as an early birthday present

---

[51] --, p. 3, --
[52] Legal Information Institute, January 2, 2015

to herself. Upcoding, fragmentation billing, and split billing are all different ways that people can leverage the complex billing codes to overcharge Medicare, a.k.a., you. One strategy that many of you could probably guess at (if you've done your homework and read the beginning of this book that is), is the falsification of medical records. Just as fraudsters can change a name from Jim to John on a tax refund form, so too can an unscrupulous medical provider alter medical records to create a new patient and justify unnecessary Medicare billing.

The healthcare system is a massive industry, with so many loop-holes and ditches that fraudsters can find to make a home in. Take the example of an elderly patient, who was hospitalized and then moved to rehabilitation care. The rehabilitation center (just across the street) sent the patient to the hospital for daily radiation therapy. The ambulance driver was given paperwork [fig. 12] for each patient he drove. This paperwork was then thrown away after the patient was dropped off at the hospital. Take a close look at all the information that was available not only to the driver, but to anyone who picked this document out of the trash.

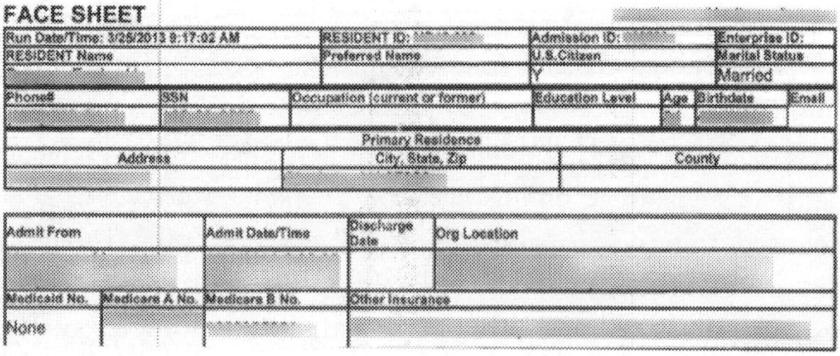

Figure 12: A document filled with sensitive information that would have been thrown away

The driver was delivering a dozen patients each day, with the same detailed form for each person. The document shows the patient's name, address, phone number, Social Security number, date of birth, and Medicare number—making it easily worth $100 or more to the seasoned fraudster. Let's pretend this driver is a potential fraudster. Let's say he makes $10.50 an hour for driving patients. If you do your math, you'll realize that the driver could easily accumulate 3,000 documents a year, earning a total street value of $300,000, if he collected and sold that paperwork, to the proper party. Driving the hospital ambulance makes him $21,000 a year *before* taxes. How many people could (and would) resist the temptation of making a total of 14 years of income just by collecting one year's worth of paperwork—which would otherwise be thrown in to the garbage?

This form had extra info that could be leveraged, including cell numbers and relationships. Perhaps this ambulance driver is a pretty clever guy. Maybe he makes a phone call to any of the immediate family listed on the lower half of the form, which included their names, cell numbers and relationship to the patient, such as a son, daughter, spouse, or even a daughter or son-in law. It would probably sound something like this: "Hello, this is FRD Rehabilitation, there is no emergency, but we just need to finish up some paperwork for your mother. Since you are listed in our paperwork as a healthcare proxy we need to have your Social Security number on file, as it's required by law." Maybe they would be extra sneaky and ask for a credit card number, in case the patient rings up any miscellaneous TV or phone charges.

Are you starting to think that paperwork shouldn't have been thrown out?

The impact of healthcare fraud will be enormous, and we say "will" because this kind fraud is just the beginning. We have seen recent hackings tied to large-scale medical institutions, but over time, we anticipate all types of medical-related identity theft to accelerate. When it comes to healthcare, you have two sides, the providers and the patients. Both want something and need something else in return. The providers have the opportunity to claim services rendered, and bill the federal government. Hospitals and doctors offices are by no means fraudsters' sole targets. A lot of fraudulent opportunities present themselves through the pharmaceutical market as well. Pharmacists are definitely not off-limits in the identity fraud game, but off label drugs aren't either. Off label drug marketing, or marketing a drug for non-FDA approved use, is another way for the medical world to get some extra dough. Along those same lines is billing Medicare for defective drugs or medical devices. At its scariest, fraudsters can go all out and just pretend to be a doctor. Who needs to go to medical school anyways? We've got WebMD!

Just ask Frank Abagnale. Frank posed as a doctor for 14 months at a hospital in Atlanta, Ga. During that time he ran the night shift of a pediatric care floor in that hospital. Frank got out of the medical business when he realized the life and death impact he could have while posing as a real doctor. Frank is not the only one either. There have been several cases of improperly certified health care professionals, and even those in practice without a high school diploma. That certainly won't help your back pain go away.

If you're curious about how much money these scams are making—you shouldn't be. if you don't already know that healthcare makes a boatload of money, then clearly you've been in living in Canada. Putting healthcare and fraud together might be the most profitable business choice a fraudster can make in this economy. In fact, in one investigation in 2012, federal officials uncovered a $375 million dollar home healthcare scam in Texas. The main operator of the scheme was charged with certifying hundreds of fraudulent claims for Medicare reimbursement, and pocketing millions in payments for services not needed, or never delivered. He allegedly hid much of his Medicare money in an offshore account in the Cayman Islands, and was apparently planning to flee there in the near future. That was further proved by his library, where he had a copy of a book called "Hide Your A$$ET$ and Disappear," and a guide to yacht registration in the Caymans.

One Los Angeles physician was indicted for a $33 million scheme to defraud Medicare. The doctor ran a medical clinic from which he billed Medicare for non-necessary medical procedures, which often were not even performed. Additionally, the man also signed prescriptions, certifications, and other medical documents for medically unnecessary home health services, hospice services, and power wheelchairs. The doctor's co-conspirators then sold the prescriptions and certifications to medical supply companies, home health agencies, and other providers. Based on these fraudulent prescriptions and certifications, the providers then allegedly submitted false and fraudulent claims to Medicare. The spree resulted in $33,484,779 in false and fraudulent claims to Medicare, of which Medicare paid approximately $22,056,332.[53] In a separate case, a doctor and a medical administrator billed Medicare $2.1 million for urinary, bowel and sexual dysfunction tests that were never performed. This fraudster pair claimed billings for 429 patients in just two months, of which 156 patients were apparently billed in only one day. Which, if it were accurate, would be roughly three minutes per patient.[54]

Patients can be fraudsters too. Patients use other identities, and bounce from doctor to doctor trying to get prescription drugs for the same ailment on multiple occasions. Additionally, Health and Human Services Office of the Inspector General reported that 8 million of the new enrollees for the new government health insurance program have applied and been approved. That may sound great until you realize that the portion of the enrollment system for verification of citizenship was never enabled, and approximately 1.3 million of the applicants cannot verify their citizenship, but are now getting government subsidized healthcare benefits.

---

[53] The United States Department of Justice, 2014
[54] Roser, 2014

In one documented case, several Russian diplomats living in New York were defrauding Medicaid, racking up almost $1.5 million in benefits. The criminal complaint stated that forty-nine diplomats and their spouses were submitting false applications, under-reporting household income, and/or making false statements concerning their children's citizenship status in order to continue their health care coverage. According to court papers, 92 percent of the births to Russian diplomats and their spouses between 2004 and 2013 in New York City were paid for by Medicaid benefits.[55]

Every case of healthcare fraud is unique, though many fall into more predictable patterns. Patients will defraud practitioners, providers will defraud the healthcare companies, and on it goes. There are many different combinations and ways in which the healthcare monster can rear its ugly head, which is just one of the reasons why healthcare fraud is so serious. Sometimes, people can get incredibly organized, and get everyone in on the fraud. Eleven people were indicted on federal charges of defrauding Medicare and Medicaid by signing up enrollees in foreign countries. The fraudsters had people living in Nicaragua and the Dominican Republic enroll in Medicare and Medicaid while listing Florida doctors as their primary care physicians. The defendants then allegedly paid for these people to travel to Florida for care, and then shared the $25.2 million that Medicare and Medicaid paid out.[56] This healthcare scheme managed to cross United States borders, and pay out benefits to non-United States residents—something that widens our minds to the infinite possibilities of United States resources being squandered as fraudsters see fit.

CARELESSNESS AND INTERNAL MISTAKES

One seemingly obvious aspect of any kind of benefit is that money should not be paid out to dead people. They simply don't need it! Just

---

[55] Dienst and Valiquette, 2013
[56] Bandell, 2014

as with government agencies, healthcare agencies are not bothering to check the Death Master File. Healthcare companies and government agencies have the tools at their fingertips to prevent "zombie beneficiaries" from receiving payments—also known as their living relatives, unscrupulous neighbors, or a whole raft of other potential criminals—but these companies are not using them. We know this because of the still constant (and more than likely rising) rate of fraudulent activity happening in the world of the dead.

"Drugs for deceased beneficiaries are clearly not medically indicated,"[57] a report from the Inspector General's office read. The report was written in response to Medicare paying for drugs after the beneficiaries had died. The report focuses on the 150 occurrences of HIV drugs being paid for after the deaths of their recipients—though the report notes that this kind of waste and abuse happens with all kinds of drugs. The report recommended the following statutes be put into place to help better regulate the dispensation of drugs and funding:

> We recommend that CMS change its practice of paying for drugs that have a date of service within 32 days after the beneficiary's death. CMS should eliminate or—if necessary for administrative processing issues—shorten the window in which it accepts PDE records for drugs dispensed after a beneficiary's death. Such a change would prevent inappropriate payments for drugs for deceased beneficiaries and lead to cost savings for the program and for taxpayers.[58]

It's frightening to realize that these measures had not *already* been in place, that it took this long for healthcare companies to start

---

[57] Murrin, 2014
[58] Murrin, p. ii, 2014

realizing that significant amounts of money can be lost due to fraudulent schemes such as this.

In response to the report, the Centers for Medicare & Medicaid Services said it would tighten its claims-processing procedure to make it more difficult for "dead people" to fill prescriptions. In 2014, Medicare and Medicaid shelled out more than $74 billion in "improper payments" alone, according to the Government Accountability Office. These are payments that should not have been made or were for an incorrect amount. Medicare's Inspector General manages to secure refunds in some cases, but tens of billions of dollars are still lost annually to fraud and waste.

America's healthcare has significant issues with regard to identity fraud, and it's only slated to get worse. The new mandate for national healthcare, the complexity of healthcare services, and all of the moving pieces within the industry, including subscribers, providers, insurers, and the government create countless opportunities for theft and fraud. As we have seen with fraud associated with SNAP, which only gives out benefits to 15 percent of the population, or 47 million people, healthcare now includes all 320 million Americans. For 2015 Medicare and Medicaid will have a combined budget of over $1 trillion dollars. The size, scope and complexity are so vast that it will surely create holes and pockets allowing all kinds of new fraud to develop. Additional, health-related programs such as the Children's Health Insurance Program (CHIP) are by no means fraud-proof, meaning that their budgets (on average $10 billion) are bleeding from fraud as well. Bank robbers used to rob banks because that's where the money was. How many banks have over a trillion dollars to steal from every year? Not many.

How to Fraud 105: Medicare and Medicaid

Medicare and Medicaid present opportunities for one of the more sophisticated forms of identity fraud. Frauding the healthcare system is one of the most lucrative schemes, as it just has so much to give. Federal healthcare has a budget over $1 trillion. The risk of being caught? Extremely low. A recent GAO report stated that these two programs lose 10% of both programs, to fraud each year. We believe the percentage of funds lost to fraud is much higher, but as with all of our defrauded programs, it is impossible to attain an accurate picture of how much money is being lost.

In this final fraud lesson, we'll discuss how to perform a complex healthcare fraud. We will try and mask the fraud within a legitimate business, making it difficult to discover. In addition, we will locate the business in an area that has a high percentage of elderly and indigent, thus making high usage of these programs believable. Additionally, we will be using stolen identities, false applications, bogus diagnoses, and false billing. In order to legitimize our operation, we will have some patients that actually benefit from the fraud. We are going to start by creating or using an existing Florida based healthcare program.

Your first question may be, "Why are we using real people? Doesn't that actually endanger our anonymity?" First of all, not everyone in the office and organization is part of the criminal operation. One of the most believable ways to operate a business is to actually operate one. In order to make it look like a legitimate business, we therefore need patients coming into the office and obtaining services. To help legitimize what we are doing, if the patients get a "Benefit" like free healthcare, we can up charge the procedures and or create totally fictitious bills for these patients. To keep the "patients" at arms length, minimizing any chance they could be questioned, we will try to use as many non-United States citizens as possible. Just like in an actual fraud that happened in a South Florida scam that resulted a theft of over $25 million. These individuals were defrauding Medicare and Medicaid by enrolling people from Nicaragua and the Dominican Republic after convincing them that they could receive benefits as citizens of those countries.[59]

Next, we will assign these individuals stolen identities so we can bill Medicare and Medicaid. All they need to do is claim to be a citizen and provide the stolen identity. By ordering additional medical services, unnecessary equipment, devices, and drugs, we'll start to run up a fairly hefty tab with the healthcare companies. If everything runs smoothly, we could operate under this scheme for about a year or two, and then quickly close up shop before the investigators come knocking. Even with the 2006 law requiring Recovery Audit Contractors (RAC), the volumes of places to search and audit are overwhelming, making it difficult for healthcare companies to stay on top of rooting out fraud within their systems.

[59] Bandell, 2014

CHAPTER FIVE

So, What Do We Do Now?

In 2014, the New Jersey Department of Labor and Workforce Development (NJLWD) prevented $4.4 million in unemployment insurance fraud over the previous year. There were approximately 646 instances of attempted identity fraud that were prevented by using an identity proofing solution, to verify and authenticate the identities of individuals applying for unemployment insurance benefits through the Labor Department's website. This new system is an important part of a larger anti-fraud program that has saved New Jersey's Labor Department nearly $450 million since 2011.

"Fraudsters steal identities and hide behind the anonymity of the Internet, taking benefits from those who need them most," said Haywood Talcove, chief executive officer of the Government Division for Risk Solutions at LexisNexis.

The economic climate is still tough on a lot of Americans, people who work hard but can't make ends meet, people with kids who have special needs, men and women living in unsafe home environments. We have no room in our federal budget for fraudsters, especially when there are individuals out there who rely upon the money that they steal.

But as New Jersey's story shows, there's hope! Just as technology has allowed fraud to grow at unprecedented rates, it's also how government agencies and individuals can fight back against the wave.

In this chapter, we've included a framework for government agencies to use to make decisions about what fraud prevention strategies to put in place. Fraud is insidious, constantly evolving, and growing rapidly in popularity and accessibility. How can we fight back as individuals, as a country? What can our government do to better its security, and ours? There are new technological advancements that government agencies can use to better safeguard their constituents' personal information and taxpayers' money.

At the end of the chapter, we have given some solutions for individuals and families. The truth is that you don't have much power against fraudsters, but you have some. Let's talk about it.

SOLUTIONS FOR GOVERNMENT AGENCIES

Protecting people's personal information should be a no-brainer. Unfortunately, it is often an afterthought. The Oakland Unified School administration abandoned their headquarters in January 2013, after a janitor left a faucet on overnight, flooding the building. In the interim, it became a haven for the homeless—and a treasure trove of personal information. At least five Oakland school employees became victims of identity theft over the course of two weeks. They blamed the district for failing to protect their payroll information, and hey, can you blame them? There were thousands of pages of sensitive documents left in the abandoned building.

The investigative team found not only records for employees, but also for students, including their addresses, birth dates and Social Security numbers. There were unemployment records, W-2s and the confidential records that the district's legal department was storing as well. All of this information was abandoned for over 18 months. During that time there were countless break-ins, ranging from shelter-seeking homeless people to teens with spray paint, and at least one identity thief. One of the victims had the entirety of his checking account withdrawn. Pretty easy pickings for your local neighborhood fraudster.

Among the five victims (that we know of) who had their identities stolen, there have been credit cards taken out, store accounts created, and inquiries into their retirement funds. After word got out about the scandal, and the lack of action on the school district's part, investigators asked to see what had been done about the problem. They were shown hundreds of boxes of now safeguarded information. Unfortunately, the response was because of the investigation in the first place. Had there been no news on the topic, those documents would probably still be floating around in the basement of the Oakland administrative office.

What this scenario shows is how little care employers and agencies take to protect employee and customer identities. What many businesses (schools included) fail to understand is that a lack of trust means a loss of business. The big picture idea goes way past one school's lost documents. If a business is seen as careless with regard to its customers' personal information, they're going to lose those customers. God forbid if their business is hacked, sales are certainly going to drop, and lots of people will have their personal information exposed.

But governments face little such pressure: Only in the court of public opinion are they judged. When there is a data breach at a government agency, the most likely consequence for the employees and the agency that should have been guarding our information is -- Nothing.

In their pursuit of efficiency and to make things easier for people, most agencies have done the equivalent of leaving buildings full of personal data.

A TIERED STRATEGY

Remember the story of Jacob and Esau from the Bible that we wrote about in the introduction? Identity theft has always been with us, since the earliest days, and it always will be. We will never eliminate it entirely. But we can fairly easily make it much harder for fraudsters to do their work.

We suggest a tiered strategy for government agencies, a series of escalating defenses that meet fraudsters every step of the way. We won't be able to plug every hole, but we will be able to significantly reduce fraud. The first step, just like in Alcoholics Anonymous, is for governments to admit they have a problem. Remember, right now, most agencies acknowledge only a tiny portion of the fraud we suspect is going on. As an example, the Federal Trade Commission, which collects fraud complaints from across the government, has said there were 369,145 "reported" complaints in 2012 -- the same year the Treasury Inspector General for Tax Administration found that 1.8 million identities had been stolen to fraud the IRS alone. That same year the Bureau of Justice estimated the number of identity thefts to be 16 million. Come on guys, let's get on the same page. Obviously a very small percentage of people are even calling the FTC to report that their identity has been compromised, so what's the point?

We know what you're thinking: This is going to cost a fortune, right? No, we don't think so. We are going to suggest an approach that allows government officials to control costs and fund security measures by savings from fraud prevention.

We can't make promises. We are just two managers who make series use of Casual Friday, who happened to uncover this issue, become passionate about it and start writing about it. But our very conservative estimate is that state and federal governments lose $26.87 billion a year to identity theft based fraud. This is about a quarter of the reported fraud, waste and abuse across major federal agencies estimated to be $109.9 billion in 2014. If you can manage to plug even some of the holes in your agency's security, and prevent some of that fraud, we suspect that you will see savings in a year or two that will enable you to keep investing.

And one of the most important parts of the solution, being open to changing the status quo and working with other government agencies, is free. The solutions we are proposing are only one line of defense. They address what the blue-collar hackers are doing: the average, cheat-the-system, apply-for-benefits 10 times fraudster. Defending against the white-collar fraudsters who hack the systems in the first place requires building up computer security walls and then constantly updating them.

First, let's get the language down. There are a variety of solutions being marketed, all under slightly different names. Following is our quick-and-dirty guide to what each one of these phrases means. If you are looking to invest in an identity proofing system, look for three qualities: identity resolution, identity verification and identity authentication.

Identity proofing systems (also known as identity verification systems) verify and authenticate the identity of legitimate customers. Identify proofing solutions also keep fraudulent users from accessing customers' data. In other words, good goes in, garbage stays out.

Identity resolution provides real-time updates to a data source(s) to confirm whether an identity exists, and whether it can be matched only to one person. It also should alert the operator to possible errors or red flags, such as a transposed Social Security number.

Identity verification capabilities identify and link separate pieces of personal information around a single identity, checking along the way to see whether all the separate pieces fit together to equal one, real, living person. Compare it to baking a cake: You search all over your kitchen for ingredients, and once you put them together, you should end up with something that's fluffy and delicious and preferably chocolate. If you end up with lasagna, however, then you clearly weren't using the correct ingredients. Identity Verification usually ties together and verifies the four key aspects of an identity: name, address, Social Security number and date of birth.

Identity authentication systems compare multiple data sources to challenge biographical information, such as former residences and vehicle history, or can incorporate data elements provided by your organization (such as prior transaction amounts and the date of last visit).

These kinds of solutions are for any and all government agencies that deal with identities. That means *all* of them. Remember, government agencies exist for the sole purpose of helping their constituents. Anything that you can do within the context of your agency to help protect their identities is paramount to the success of the agency itself—and to keeping your citizens safe.

Here is what a real-world approach could look like.

The easiest, simplest, cheapest approach is a quiz given to applicants for government benefits and licenses. Some financial services companies have begun implementing these systems. The idea is that you ask, either verbally or in a Q&A format online, a series of multiple choice or True/False questions, like, "At which one of these addresses did you once live?" The answers are then matched to the data record that matches the name the applicant has given. The difficulty here is that people taking the quiz range from Forrest Gump to Einstein -- but that's why you have a tiered system, to help the Forrests get the benefits they need, if they fail the quiz.

The second tier of the system, for applicants that fail the quiz, is a requirement that they submit a two-sided picture of their drivers' licenses, including the 2D barcode. The barcode contains all the information that is written on the license, and again could be matched with the agencies' database. This isn't as complicated as it might sound: Think about how ubiquitous selfies have become. Taking two images of a drivers' license is no more complicated than two selfies, but a lot more useful.

The beauty of a tiered approach is that you can use the cheapest solution -- the quiz -- for the most people. At each point, the number of people who fail the tests will get smaller, so that your agency doesn't need to apply the most expensive solutions to the greater numbers of people.

Finally, the highest and smallest tier is to look at the identifying information of the computer's IP address or other identifying information on a mobile device. If an application purportedly from a woman in Kentucky is coming from an IP address in Bulgaria, the system flags the application.

An agency could, at any point in this tiered system, decide to call it quits on the applicant: If you fail to answer your questions correctly on the quiz, you could be rejected. We suggest that this is too difficult, however. The instinct that led many agencies to open up their applications' processes and make them easier for people was a good instinct. Being jerked around by a bureaucracy is cruel and unusual punishment. That's why the final tiers, especially for critical programs such as food stamps and drivers' licenses, should be phone calls and an in-person visit to the agency. Some of the best fraud prevention programs are human conversations and face-to-face contact.

In addition to being tiered, the system is also multi-dimensional. That means at the same time a process is checking an application against a data file, data is also being crosschecked and updated across other agencies' information.

Does this sound complicated? We suggest agencies develop downloadable apps to gather information from applicants. The apps can be updated continually to keep up with the fraudsters' advances, too.

Some agencies are already having success with some of the strategies we suggest.

SOLUTIONS SPOTLIGHT: THE DEPARTMENT OF MOTOR VEHICLES

In our opinion, the government agencies most in need of new solutions are the Department of Motor Vehicles, a.k.a. The Registry of Motor Vehicles, a.k.a. The Bureau of Motor Vehicles. Regardless of what you call it, the state agencies that oversee vehicle registrations and licensing are difficult to regulate, and critically important. This is a challenging responsibility for states, which have varied laws and enforcement. Overseeing and enforcing driver testing, license issuance, vehicle registration, and suspensions and revocation makes for a fairly complicated operation. Add in the new requirements, such as the licensing of illegal aliens, the constant demand to cut costs and laborers, and the need to reduce wait times for impatient people. DMVs are under a lot of pressure.

Of all of the responsibilities tied to a Department of Motor Vehicles, the most important is the verification and authentication of an individual's identity when issuing a license. To a fraudster's drivers' license with photo that matches his or her face and information that won't trigger any concerns is one of the Holy Grails of identity theft.

The terrorists of 9/11 were not the only ones who understood the power of having valid identification. In November 2012, a foreign student was convicted in Texas for the attempted use of a weapon of mass destruction. The man planned to attack nuclear power plants, reservoirs, dams, and New York City streets during rush hour. His plan outlined several steps on how to carry out his mission, one of which included obtaining a forged United States birth certificate in order to apply for a United States passport and multiple valid drivers' licenses. The student lacked only a single chemical needed to complete his explosives before the FBI arrested him.[60]

A driver's license enables the holder a variety of privileges by linking the displayed "identity"—name, address, and date of birth—in conjunction with the picture on that license. A license is used to verify age, driving privileges, travel abilities, and can be used to obtain documents such as passports, birth certificates, and Social Security cards. Additionally, licenses are also legitimate forms

---

[60] PR Newswire, 2013

of identification used to create bank accounts, obtain student loans, buy property and/or vehicles, order credit cards, and even file for government benefits. Issuing a license with the picture of one person and the identity of another person becomes a huge gateway to identity theft, and is the basic building block to downstream fraud and deception. There are a variety of reasons why an individual would pose as someone else, or to try and obtain a second license. Here are a few:

- Desire to travel under the guise of a different, or even legal, citizen. For example, an individual may be on a national or terrorist watch list. A drivers' license allows him or her to go undetected at the airport.

- To gain government benefits such as unemployment, food stamps, housing, etc.

- To help illegal aliens to stay in the United States under a false identity and to drive and travel.

- To buy or obtain a car, truck, or property under another name for criminal intent.

- To rent a property as a drug drop house

- To enable driving while faced with a suspended or revoked license

- Hide from law enforcement (actually taking on the stolen identity full-time).

- A commercial license holder wants a backup license in case of DUIs or tickets, thus protecting his livelihood.

- To enable underage drinking.

The reasons listed above for wanting to obtain a first, second, or even a third license under another identity are just a few of many. With additional licenses, or "identities," criminals and terrorists can move about with anonymity, thus cloaking their plans and efforts via someone else's identity and helping them to defraud, and even harm, U.S. citizens. The challenge facing licensing agencies is that they are tasked with determining identities often with incomplete, inaccurate, and misleading information.

A 2012 GAO report studied the methods of surrendering a current license from one state and obtaining a new license from a second state. The GAO had fraudulent licenses created and used them to obtain new licenses in a second state. All three states accepted, and never checked the validity of the surrendered licenses. Thus they traded a fake for a real license, and allowed the fake identity to pass onto the new license along with the photo of the imposter. *The GAO went on to say that this is a significant flaw in the cross border system, but that it will not be fixed until 2023.*

There's one more thing to worry about when it comes to driver's licenses. The most basic element of becoming licensed to operate a vehicle is taking and passing both the written and physical driving test. Illegally procured licenses placed in the wrong hands create a true hazard to public safety, as they have not taken the necessary tests, and might be dangerous drivers. The avoidance of a license suspension or revocation through the use of a secondary license again puts the public at risk. Underage drinking and driving is another issue. Criminals can also use fictitious licenses to hide their identities, thus avoiding arrest, and enabling the activity to continue, in every vein from hitting the bars at age 18 to disguising yourself as a government affiliate when you are not. Imagine what those consequences could be.

Often, people are not too concerned over fake IDs, thinking that the worst thing that could happen is an underage kid buys a couple of beers. The answer is that lots of pretty fake looking fake IDs are accepted as legitimate all the time at college bars and restaurants everywhere. The issue is that fake IDs are becoming better and better. In October 2014, hundreds of thousands of fake IDs were shipped in from China. These fakes are so real that they are confounding the experts, who can't seem to tell the difference. It is not the fake-looking fake IDs you remember from your college days that are the bigger problem here—it's the ones that can fool the specialists that we have to worry about.[61] And there are many, many of those.

SOLVING THE DMV PROBLEM

Most Departments of Motor Vehicles use the Social Security Administration's Social Security number as the recognized identifier for United States citizens and legal aliens. The Social Security number ties an individual's name, date and place of birth together to create an identity that is supposed to be unique. Recently the Social Security number system changed so that Social Security numbers are random sequences of numbers, as opposed to elements of your personal information, thus eliminating the ability to determine a Social Security number based on the above factors. Over the last 10 years, theft and misuse of Social Security numbers has become commonplace and the once unique Social Security number is no longer valid. Identity fraud is the basis for the majority of crimes being perpetrated against government programs through the misuse of stolen Social Security numbers. So what then, can we do? If the base-line identifier is no longer applicable, what other systems can the Department of Motor Vehicles (and other government agencies)

---

[61] Savini, 2014

implement on a national level to help eliminate fraud within their agencies?

The answer lies in identity proofing solutions to help trace citizens through the many changes life brings (moving, name changes, etc.). Remember, identities are dynamic. People move, change their names and have children. Identity proofing solutions help mitigate that, and keep people as people, instead of a string of identifying numerical codes. Identity proofing solutions are starting to be recognized as one of the best ways of verifying identities. In Logan International Airport in Boston, a new identity proofing solution has recently put in to be sure that the person walking through the airport is the same person whose name is on their ticket, and who is the same person on his or her license. This technology analyses the space between facial features of a given person with a real-time photo and their photo identification that they are carrying with them. The photograph, identification, and individual are then analyzed by an agent to be sure there were no mistakes.

SUCCESS STORIES FROM FACIAL RECOGNITION TECHNOLOGY AND IDENTITY-PROOFING SYSTEMS

A convicted armed-robber eluded authorities for almost 41 years after escaping from prison. But with the help of facial recognition technology, he was caught living in northeastern Iowa under the identities of two 5-year-old boys who had died in the 1940s. The man spent decades evading detection after escaping from a now-closed prison in Huntersville, N.C., in 1973. He used the identities of Louie Vance and William Henry Cox for years as he traveled from Chicago to Georgia to Washington State to Iowa. He convinced the Social Security Administration to grant him disability and retirement benefits under both names for years. After moving to Iowa, however, facial recognition software used by Iowa's government systems since 2008, flagged Carnes' photo after he applied for a license in Vance's name. The face appeared to be the same man who had obtained an Iowa license last year under Cox's name. Identity-proofing systems have yielded some pretty convincing results—and some pretty incredible stories. This kind of facial recognition technology solves issues such as Boundary Blindness, and allows officials to search for fugitives and criminals based solely on something a little more permanent than a name: their face.

Another story to give you some hope for the future is that of the capture of a convicted sex offender who had been living under another name. The man knew a woman who had been a former hospital nurse, and she created fake prenatal and birth records to help him obtain a new identity and Social Security card. While he was living under a new name, he did not, obviously, register as a sex offender. Luckily, facial recognition software was there to save the day. The state motor vehicles department database where he lived found a likely match between the man's new ID card image and his old drivers license photo. The Inspector General's office was alerted and an investigation began, which uncovered that the two men were one and the same.[62]

The successes don't stop at individual stories either—more than $78 million in wrongfully requested tax refunds was blocked by the Indiana Department of Revenue in 2014, thanks to the department's increased security activities,[63] and a nifty database called the Tax Data Warehouse. This sounds quite possibly like the most boring place on the planet, but it might've saved your butt once or twice, so don't knock it quite yet.

A Tax Data Warehouse is a database that contains the tax returns for a state or federal government, and is usually used for income tax purposes. A state needs to store and keep track of filed tax returns and to index them by name, income levels, and other factors. These databases have all of their citizens' financial information, bits

---

[62] The Associated Press, 2013
[63] Indiana Department of Revenue, 2014

and pieces that usually span many years. Again, we see that identities are dynamic, not static. In order to catalogue these large amounts of information in any sensible order, the Tax Data Warehouse must be able to track changes for specific individuals over time. Moving, name changes, you know the drill. Now the Tax Data Warehouses have built-in rules that help them look for fraud and errors.

Thus, when Alicia claims she made $100,000 last year but wants a $10,000,000 refund, the system throws a flag and pulls out the return so someone can review it. There are lots of different catches that can be programmed into these systems, so that they can automatically look for anomalies. If Bill is claiming 10 children as dependents in 2014, when in the last year he only claimed two, the system will flag it.

Indiana taxpayers who took an Identity Confirmation Quiz to help the department confirm their identities reported it was easy for most, quick to take, and many expressed appreciation for the additional level of protection. In comparison with 1,500 manually blocked identity theft cases in 2013, the department's Special Investigations Unit confirmed more than 74,000 returns with bad identities in the 2014 tax year.

It seems that regardless of location, type of fraud, or demographic, fraud rates, in all respects, are rising. There is no way around the numbers, but there are tools being put in place to help stabilize and lower them. Facial recognition technology uses biometric measurements between facial features of an individual, such as the distance between the pupils, combined with the distance from each pupil to the tip of the nose or the chin. With enough measurements, each face becomes more and more mathematically unique. At the end of the day new technologies and many not listed here are going to be the key to resolving this fraud problem.

REDUCING POST-DISASTER FRAUD

We are highlighting post-disaster fraud because it's both a weak point in the system and a place where we particularly want to get things right. People who are the victims of hurricanes, floods, tornadoes or other disasters need our help, quickly. But we don't want to see people masquerading as victims get help they don't need.

The same rules of thumb for committing any other kind of identity fraud apply here too. A form for emergency assistance can be tampered with, duplicated, or entirely fabricated with personal information that has been stolen or altered. A real resident of an affected area may claim damages that never occurred, or can claim a property, as his own that actually is not. The options are endless—and because payments must be made quickly, sometimes things get overlooked. As noted in a statement to a subcommittee on disaster recovery, the Federal Emergency Management Association (FEMA) must find a way to "balance the requirement to quickly distribute funds to meet the needs of disaster survivors with its responsibility to be good stewards of taxpayer funds."[64] FEMA is seeking out this balance through both recouping old overpayments and also working to keep better track of payments in the first place.

After Hurricane Katrina, the fraud rate rocketed and was estimated at $1 billion. After Katrina, FEMA realized that measures were needed to insure more stringent payment measures and to verify identities of those filing for disaster benefits. The first step FEMA took was to investigate possible fraudulent (or mistaken) overpayments. As of Dec. 31, 2010, over $3 million was collected in restitution payments that were paid out after Hurricanes Katrina and Rita.[65] Between 2006 and 2010, FEMA instituted a Fraud Prevention Unit, which has investigated nearly 3,200 disaster fraud complaints and referred more than 2,400 fraud cases to the Office

[64] Zimmerman, p. 2, 2011
[65] Zimmerman, p. 2, 2011

of the Inspector General for investigation or review. This unit has managed to keep millions in disaster payments from being improperly disbursed since its institution. These measures, and others, have managed to reduce the fraud rate related to natural disasters from 14.5 percent to less than 3 percent.

Even the GAO seems to be impressed with FEMA's response to fraudulent claims: "[s]ince Hurricanes Katrina and Rita, FEMA has improved its controls over identity and address verification and inspections, housing assistance in FEMA-paid hotels, and duplicate registrations. Improvements in these three key areas have reduced FEMA's risk of making payments based on fraudulent disaster assistance registrations."[66]

The other half of FEMA's measures to reduce agency-related fraud are to stop it before it begins. It's much easier to not pay out money in the first place rather than to collect money after its been paid, especially if the recipients are intentionally frauding the system, and are apt to disappear after they've received their check. Elizabeth Zimmerman, FEMA's associate administrator of the Office of Response and Recover Associate Administrator, described how any unusual activity, from an inappropriate change in an applicant's bank account number to improper attempts to gain access to secure databases, will be identified in real time.[67] According to Zimmerman, the specific steps FEMA has taken to insure proper payments range from instant verification of an individual through cross-checking personal information (such as their name, address, Social Security number, and date of birth) and "high risk" mailing addresses, such as jails and cemeteries, are barred from receiving automated payments, to online submissions being monitored for duplication.[68] All these measures, and others, are all excellent steps

---

[66] GAO-09-671 June 2009

[67] Zimmerman, p. 6, 2011

[68] Zimmerman, p. 7, 2011

to helping reduce fraudulent claims made to take advantage of a potentially life-saving social service.

While fraud is happening everywhere, all the time, some days are certainly worse than others. Natural disasters provide a serious distraction, allowing lots of opportunities to fraud the system. A large part of the problem with identity fraud resulting from natural disasters is that there is not a lot of time from when a disaster strikes to when the applications start flooding in to check up on peoples' claims. The goal for assistance-based agencies is to get funds to the people who need it most—and fraudsters have tapped into the system. Luckily, FEMA's efforts over the last several years have given the fraudsters a run for their money.

SOLUTIONS FOR INDIVIDUALS AND FAMILIES

Somehow, the lesson about not giving a stranger your personal information was left out in favor of the one about looking both ways before you cross the street. The single most important thing you can do to protect your identity is to keep your personal information private. Many schools, doctors' offices, dentists' offices, colleges, and job applications ask for your Social Security number simply because it's on the form. That doesn't mean you need to fill it in.

These forms are a template that almost anyone can download online. If you are filling out a form, for instance, and it asks for your Social Security number, either leave that space blank, or directly ask the secretary what that information will be used for. If someone cannot provide you with a sufficient answer, don't write your personal information down. In most cases your SSN will not be used for anything more than filling the space on the form, so if it isn't used to check for credit and they insist, fill it with all zeros or all ones. The employee collecting the form may say "that's not your social." Your reply should be "How do you know?"

Thanks to the Patriot Act it is required to supply an ITIN or SSN when opening a bank account. Banks are one of the few places that you cannot get away with leaving the space blank or filling in a blatantly bogus number.

In many banks, employees will ask for the last four digits of your Social Security number to verify your identity. If you mention that you're uncomfortable giving out such sensitive information, you'll merely be asked for your driver's license instead.

Many people feel as if they can't deny information for fear of not receiving services, especially the elderly. We can almost guarantee that whatever company you are trying to use will not deny you service for not putting down your Social Security number. If employees get aggressive, stand up for yourself! This is your personal information. If you're filling out a form on a website that marks the Social Security number as a mandatory field, call the company or agency and ask why they need that information specifically, who will see it, and what it will be used for. If they cannot provide a sufficient answer, ask if there is another piece of identifying information they could use instead. A lot is at stake when it comes to your Social Security number—don't give it up so easily.

Another way of protecting yourself is to be very wary of potential phishing scams. Very few legitimate websites for legitimate businesses, banks, universities, etc. will ask for your personal information through an e-mail or a text message. If you think a spammer is contacting you, report it to the legitimate website's help hotline or e-mail address. Remember also to make sure that government websites end in .gov. If the domain ends in anything else, be wary. False government websites have been on the rise in fraud scams, and they're designed to look realistic. Make sure to have antivirus software installed on your computer to help protect you from viruses and information-grabbing technologies.

What about credit monitoring? It's good to monitor your credit, but it's better to monitor your Social Security number. Credit monitoring alone cannot protect you from synthetic identity theft -- remember, that's the theft that happens when someone has used part of your identity, like your Social Security number, to construct a new identity that's used to claim benefits. Credit monitoring services are now starting to monitor Social Security number use as an enhanced service, and signing up is a good idea.

Be sure to check your annual Social Security earnings reports for mistakes (which means being up to date so you can detect these errors early). Especially, look to see if you are not getting credit on the earnings you know you've had. But be aware that only the wages reported using the correct name and Social Security number are tied to your account. Thus, someone who is using your Social Security number under another name will not appear on the report.

There are thousands of workers who pay taxes using the wrong Social Security number every year. And while some of this comes from so-called "fat-finger errors," much of it comes from illegal immigrants looking to get work, a phenomenon that some people are calling "immigrant identity theft." If your Social Security number is used illegally to gain employment, you could end up owing taxes on wages you didn't earn or have a lien placed on your assets if federal income taxes are not paid, among other consequences.

When you're deciding between identity monitoring services, be sure to select a program that will search public records for evidence of variations in your name and Social Security number and evidence that your number has become associated with different names. It's not exactly an ideal Friday afternoon, but taking time to get this stuff right could be the best decision you ever make. Some of the identity monitoring services on the market include LifeLock, Identity Guard, Identity Force, Privacy Guard, Fast 3 Credit Score, TransUnion, Free Scores and More, True Credit, My Score, My Free Score Now, Free Score 360, ID Shield, Protect My ID and ID Watchdog.

When it comes to identity fraud, children are huge targets. Taking their personal information is like, well, taking candy from a baby. Be sure to talk with your children about the importance of their Social Security number, what it means, and why keeping it private is important. Explain that they should never give out their Social Security number without your permission, and have them memorize it instead of keeping it written down or saved in their phone. Keep an eye on their credit periodically to make sure someone hasn't stolen their identity and is using it to rack up debt your child will have to deal with later in life. Explain to them that the Internet is an easy place to get into trouble, and that they should never give out personal information online. This includes keeping their full birthday and address off Facebook, Twitter, Instagram, and other social media sites.

CONCLUSION

Fraudsters stealing government benefits are not just stealing from the people who actually need it; they're stealing from you as well! Government benefit money is supposedly given to people in need because of their circumstances, including veterans, the elderly, people with disabilities or students. These are situations and circumstances that we have as a society decided deserve our support. You can argue about how much, or how to define those groups of people, but there's no question that we're better off when government support is available for people who are truly in need.

Yet, every time a fraudster scams the system he or she not only costs the government money, the fraud takes a toll on trust. After a while, you start to think that everybody who is getting government support is crooked. Remember the chief executive officer of a satellite television and broadband services company and his wife, the dog-breeder living on their yacht and receiving public assistance benefits? After you hear a few too many of those stories, your faith in the system breaks down.

Mass data breaches, and any other kind of fraud that compromises a company or government agency's customers, take another toll on trust. According to the NCL/Javelin study, which includes surveys of fraud victims from Miami, Los Angeles, Chicago, and Minneapolis, along with additional Javelin research on national fraud trends, there is a serious backlash when customers don't feel safe giving their personal information to their favorite store. For example, 59 percent of respondents whose data was breached at a retailer expressed "significantly decreased" trust in retailers who failed to protect their information. Businesses rely wholly on consumer trust—especially when a significant portion of their profits comes from online shoppers.

We also must consider how this affects government benefits. If we look at credit protection companies, they only protect you on the credit side; they have no involvement with government benefits. Bank robbers go to the bank because they want the money there, the money that's physically in the bank. But what fraudsters understand is that the real big money lies in government. The United States can print money—unfathomable amounts of money with minimal oversight and understanding of recipients. If the government has no idea who they're awarding money to, how do they know if those are real people, children, dead people, or even fake people? Answer: they don't.

Since so much identity theft goes unreported, the actual amount is unknown. You've read our estimate. We believe the government loses $26.87 billion a year to fraud that is tied to identity theft. That's probably a low estimate.

So why should you care? You should care because you, your mother, and even Big Brother are all in this together. Not only is our government being bilked. If your identity hasn't already been stolen and used, it will be.

Take the case of Derek Parks, a friend of ours and a vice president at LexisNexis. This year, he submitted his taxes on April 14 and received an immediate rejection.

"I was traveling, and I thought I needed to do was recheck my information while I was at the airport. Then I'm in the Atlanta airport the day before April 15th, trying to figure out what to do next."

Going to the IRS web site wasn't much help; he couldn't figure out what was wrong. As a stopgap, he filed for an extension. He tried for several weeks to get through to the IRS to figure out what the problem with his return was. "Facing hour-long phone calls, I gave up," he said. Eventually, he figured it out: someone had already filed for a tax return under his name. The IRS eventually cleared the return from his file but beyond that, there isn't much he can do except watch and wait to see if his identity is used for other purposes, like credit card fraud. He filed a police report and was told that his ID had most likely been stolen in a data breach at Anthem that affected as many as 80 million records.

Maybe the most shocking thing about this story to us is that Derek wasn't surprised ... at all. "Having worked in my industry for so many years, I live by the belief that everyone's identity has been compromised. It's just what I know to be true," he said. "You become a little de-sensitized. You still experience the anger and frustration. If it's this clear, why don't they do something about it?"

If the solutions seem complicated, it means you've read this book wrong. Or upside-down. Or maybe our vocabulary is at a higher-level than we thought... but in truth, we don't think that's it. We're pretty basic and the concept here is simple. People are stealing from the government and are not being held accountable for it. They are assuming identities that are either fake or belong to someone else, and using them to claim benefits from the government, make a profit from others who are, or to gain other privileges. These privileges can range from a fake ID for an underage kid to buy alcohol to boarding a plane while on a terrorist watch list to applying and receiving government benefits. In all of these cases, the bottom line is that this kind of activity is eroding our economy, in some cases creating dangerous situations, and in all cases, illegal.

Many of the agencies that are being stolen from, like the DMV's and Social Services departments, are a hotbed for fraudulent activity, a door, so to speak, into the world of identity fraud. If you manage to fraud your way into one of these agencies in particular, you start to create a legitimized "identity," making it even easier to access benefits from other agencies. These doorway agencies are just the beginning.

While technology may have been one of fraudsters' biggest assets, it is also the tool we can use to fight back to take control over our own identities once again. Technologies are being developed every day to help better protect consumers and constituents, especially facial recognition technology and identity proofing solutions. Other solutions that use biometric data, such as voiceprints, are also rising in popularity. Major banks and other large-scale institutions have implemented voice printing as a way of screening for blacklisted criminals—and making sure that callers are who they say they are. One analyst from a technology research center estimates that by 2015, 25 major United States call centers will be using some form of voiceprint technology, five times as many as the previous year.[69]

But the government won't ever make a serious attempt to fight identity theft until people in power acknowledge how serious the problem is. When our government sectors and programs recognize fraud within their agencies, those in charge must take some responsibility for the loss of taxpayer funds. It's not a fun reckoning, but it needs to be done. Waste and abuse at the hands of identity fraudsters is only getting worse. Agencies in charge of providing benefits to citizens are getting taken advantage of, and to a degree that these agencies are unaware of. Claiming a fraud rate of 1 percent—for any institution—is absurd, and helps no one. The first step to fixing the problem is to recognize that the problem exists.

Certain agencies have it worse than others, to be sure, and the agencies struggle to safeguard their technologies, which were implemented in a well-meaning but reckless effort to make it easier for constituents to get what they need. Tax refund fraud has skyrocketed, as have Social Security fraud, student loan, and unemployment fraud. Fraudsters are also taking advantage of the national healthcare

[69] Satter, 2014

system. According to the Ponemon Institute, in the last two years, 90 percent of health care companies had at least one data breach.[70] How long is it going to take us, especially our government representatives, to realize that any percentage of major data breaches is too many?

The solutions we propose in this book are a start. This book also serves to attract the attention of the individuals who run government agencies to get the word out there: Identity fraud is a serious problem, and it needs attention now.

There is little accountability in the realm of government fraud and identity theft. It is considered a "safe crime," meaning that there is a low-level of punishment, if there is a punishment at all. We weren't lying about all those drug dealers, they're still out there, they're just making a lot more money these days. Fraud is the ever-evolving, highly adaptable crime of the century. As long as we can keep just a little ahead of the curve, we can save our government agencies billions. We can help people on government benefits get the assistance they need, and we can keep American dollars where they belong. Want to do your part? Stop giving your Social Security number to the cable guy who needs it 'to verify your identity.' If your cable company is doing a better job of verifying identities than our government, we know we have a bigger problem.

When Frank Abagnale was pulling cons, they were far more intricate. They involved a full-body effort: a winning smile, a swaggering walk, and a quick tongue, and they only yielded one false identity at a time.

The way Frank Abagnale stole identities reminds us of the way the Greeks in the film *300* fought their enemy. By holing up in a narrow pass, the massive army only had as much might as the few individuals fighting in the front. Now, that pass has widened, and a whole army has gotten through. We cannot fight identity fraud single-file anymore, we are facing a much bigger, and faster evolving

---

[70] Kelly, 2015

army than our government can handle. Fraudsters have the ability to Costco shop for identities: in bulk. We need to find solutions that narrow the pass again, without cutting people off from their resources, or slowing down the speed at which our government agencies function. At the same time, however, if we do not do something soon, the fraudsters will blot out the sun.

BIBLIOGRAPHY

Bandell, Brian. "Eleven Indicted for Signing Up Foreigners for Medicare in $25M Fraud ." *South Florida Business Journal.* American City Business Journals. November 19, 2014. http://www.bizjournals.com/southflorida/news/2014/11/19/eleven-indicted-for-signing-up-foreigners-for.html?page=all (accessed January 5, 2015).

Be'ery, Tal. "The South Carolina Data Breach: A Lesson in Deaf and Blind Cybersecurity." *Security Week.* Wired Business Media. November 8, 2012. http://www.securityweek.com/south-carolina-data-breach-lesson-deaf-and-blind-cybersecurity (accessed July 1, 2014).

Brennan, Paul. "Feds have no idea the extent of SNAP fraud, says Iowa official," *Watchdog.Org* http://www.Watchdog.Org/169883/snap-fraud-iowa/ September 11th, 2014

Bureau of Justice Statistics. *16.6 Million People Experienced Identity Theft in 2012.* Release, Washington, D.C.: The Office of Justice Programs, 2013.

Collinson, Patrick. "Don't Bank on Your Phone--It Could Be Hacked by Zeus 'Trojan Horse'." *The Guardian.* July

22, 2011. http://www.theguardian.com/money/2011/jul/22/ smartphones-hacked-zeus-malware (accessed June 14, 2014).

Croteau, Scott J. "Report finds $1.6M in Tenant Fraud at Worcester Housing Authority." *Telegram.com.* Telegram & Gazette. January 23, 2013. http://www.telegram.com/article/20130123/NEWS/101239883&Template=printart (accessed January 29, 2015).

Davis, Matt. "How Much Is Your Identity Worth...on the Black Market?" *Identity Theft Resource Center.* June 24, 2013. http://www.idtheftcenter.org/Privacy-Issues/how-much-is-your-identity-worth-on-the-black-market.html (accessed June 14, 2014).

Daily News. "Man who 'dressed up as his mother for six years to steal $115,000 in benefits' faces 25 years in prison." April 23, 2012.

Dienst, Jonathan, and Joe Valiquette. "Dozens of Russian Diplomats in NY Defrauded Medicaid System: Prosecutors." *NBC New York.* LLC NBCUniversal Media. December 5, 2013. http://www.nbcnewyork.com/news/local/ Russian-Diplomat-Defraud-Health-Care-Medicaid-System-Prosecutor-US-Court-Arrest-United-Nations-234599031.html (accessed January 5, 2015).

Federal Trade Commission. *Security in Numbers, SSNs and ID Theft.* Release, Washington, D.C., 2007.

Food and Nutrition Service. "Supplemental Nutrition Assistance Program: Average Monthly Participation (Persons)." *FNS.USDA.GOV.* November 7, 2014. http://www.

fns.usda.gov/sites/default/files/pd/15SNAPpartPP.pdf (accessed December 3, 2014).

———. "Supplemental Nutrition Assistance Program: State Activity Report, Fiscal Year 2013." *FNS.USDA.GOV.* Program Accountability and Administration Division. July 1, 2014. http://www.fns.usda.gov/sites/default/files/snap/2013-state-activity.pdf (accessed December 3, 2014).

Fowle, Dana. "Department of Education threatens to dock man's social security check." Fox 5 News, Atlanta. July 13, 2015. http://www.fox5atlanta.com/news/2598897-story (accessed Oct. 13, 2015).

George, The Honorable J. Russell. *Tax-Related Identity Theft: An Epidemic Facing Seniors and Taxpayers.* Testimony, Office of the Inspector General for Tax Administration, Washington, D.C.: United States Senate, 2013, 17.

Giles, Jim. "Cyber Crime Made Easy." *New Scientist Archive* 205, no. 2752 (2010).

Goel, Vindu, and James C. McKinley Jr. "Forced to Hand Over Data, Facebook Files Appeal." *NYTimes.com.* The New York Times. June 26, 2014. http://www.nytimes.com/2014/06/27/technology/facebook-battles-manhattan-da-over-warrants-for-user-data.html?_r=1 (accessed June 29, 2014).

Harrington, Elizabeth. "Social Security paid the dead $47M, says audit." *Washington Free Beacon.* June 25, 2015.

Indiana Department of Revenue. "State Stops $78 Million in Illegitimate Tax Refunds." *Indiana Department of*

Revenue. September 2, 2014. http://www.in.gov/dor/5193.htm (accessed June 21, 2014).

Journal of Accountancy. "TIGTA, Congress Target Identity Theft." *JournalofAccountancy.com.* August 1, 2012. http://www.journalofaccountancy.com/Issues/2012/Aug/ Identity-theft.htm (accessed December 16, 2014).

Kelly, Robin. "Protecting Medical Identity Is a Must-Win Battle in the War for Cybersecurity | Commentary." *Roll Call.* Feb 12, 2015. http://www.rollcall.com/news/protecting_medical_identity_is_a_must_win_battle_in_the_war_for-240066-1.html (accessed June 6, 2015).

Legal Information Institute. *Health Care Fraud: An Overview.* Cornell University Law School. -- --, --. http://www.law.cornell.edu/wex/healthcare_fraud (accessed January 2, 2015).

Main, Frank. "The Watchdogs: Chinatown license fraud ring put dangerous drivers on the street." *Chicago Sun-Times.* Dec. 11, 2012.

Martinez, Julia. Rutledge, Patricia. Sher,Kenneth. *"Fake ID Ownership and Heavy Drinking in Underage College Students."* Health and Human Services, Washington D.C.:PMCID: PMC2711502 (July 16, 2009)

Michael R. Phillips, Deputy Inspector General for Audi. *Processes Are Not Sufficient to Minimize Fraud and Ensure the Accuracy of Tax Refund Direct Deposits.* 2008-40-182, Washington, D.C.: Treasury Inspector General for Tax Administration, 2008.

Murrin, Suzanne. *Medicare Paid for HIV Drugs for Deceased Beneficiaries.* OEI-02-11-00172, Department of
Health and Human Services, Washington D.C.: Office of Inspector General, 2014, 15.

Nguyen, Hoa. *Cops: Pelham Woman Accused of Stealing $10G after Facebook Post.* Gannett. October 23, 2014.
http://www.lohud.com/story/news/local/westches-ter/2014/10/23/pelham-woman-accused-identity-theft-face-book-post/17784657/ (accessed December 9, 2014).

Office of the Inspector General. "Ohio Woman Sentenced for Using 50 Stolen Identities to Collect Government
Benefits." *Office of the Inspector General.* Social Security Administration. August 9, 2013. http://oig.ssa.gov/audits-and-in-vestigations/investigations/aug9-ohio (accessed June 6, 2014).

Office, The United States Attorney's. *Detroit Man Sentenced for Wire Fraud and Identity Theft Fraudulent Tax
Returns Filed for Deceased Individuals.* Press Release, Eastern District of Michigan, Detroit: U.S. Department of Justice, 2014.

Ostwalt, Phil. "Country Profile: United States." *KMPG.com.* KMPG International. January 1, 2013.
http://www.kpmg.com/Global/en/IssuesAndInsights/ArticlesPublications/global-profiles-of-the-fraudster/Documents/united-states.pdf (accessed December 9, 2014).

Pagliery, Jose. ""Half of American Adults Hacked This Year."." *CNNMoney.* New York: CNN, May 28, 2014.

--. ""Hospital Network Hacked, 4.5 Million Records Stolen."." *CNNMoney.* CNN. August 18, 2014.

http://money.cnn.com/2014/08/18/technology/security/hospital-chs-hack/ (accessed June 8, 2014).

Ponemon Institute. *Fourth Annual Benchmark Study on Patient Privacy & Data Security*. Research Report, --: Sponsored by ID Experts, 2014.

PR Newswire. *Prevent Terrorists from Using Fake IDs. It is Way Overdue*. September 11, 2013. http://www.prnewswire.com/news-releases/prevent-terrorists-from-using-fake-ids-it-is-way-overdue-223276291.html (accessed December 9, 2014).

Reagan, Kevin. ""Food Stamp Fraud Costing Taxpayers Billions."." *The Daily Signal*. December 9, 2011. http://dailysignal.com/2011/12/09/food-stamp-fraud-costing-taxpayers-billions/ (accessed June 14, 2014).

Roberts, Christine. "Woman Arrested for Falsely Claiming $2.1 Million in Tax Refund." *NYDailyNews.com*. New York Dailey News. June 10, 2012. http://www.nydailynews.com/news/national/woman-arrested-falsely-claiming-2-1-million-tax-refund-article-1.1093171 (accessed December 4, 2014).

Roser, Mary Ann. "Jury Convicts Austin Doctor of $2.1 Million in Medicare Fraud." *Statesman*. November 5, 2014. http://www.statesman.com/news/news/jury-convicts-austin-doctor-of-21-million-in-medic/nh2Kz/#__federated=1 (accessed January 5, 2015).

Satter, Raphael. "Voiceprints: Banks Go High-Tech to Fight Identity Theft." *DailyFinance.com*. Jeff Horwitz.

October 13, 2014. http://www.dailyfinance.com/2014/10/13/
banks-voiceprints-fight-identity-theft/ (accessed October 14, 2014).

Savini, Dave. *2 Investigators: China Floods U.S. With Near-
Perfect Fake Driver's Licenses.* CBS Local Media.
September 22, 2014. http://chicago.cbslocal.com/2014/09/22/2-
investigators-china-floods-u-s-with-near-perfect-fake-drivers-li-
censes/ (accessed December 9, 2014).

Silvestrini, Elaine. *Tax fraud 'queen' sentenced to 21 years.* The
Tampa Tribune. July 16, 2013.
http://tbo.com/news/crime/tax-fraud-queen-sentenced-to-21-
years-20130716/ (accessed January 15, 2015).

Stein, Jason and Patrick Marley. *State mistake puts thousands
at risk of identity theft.* Milwaukee Journal Sentinel. July 24, 2102.

Sullivan, Bob. "9/11 Report Light on ID Theft Issues." *Security
on NBC News.com.* NBC News. August 4, 2004.
http://www.nbcnews.com/id/5594385/ns/us_news-security/t/
report-light-id-theft#.VDm_AUvBFuY (accessed June 14, 2014).

The Associated Press. *Prison Guard Guilty of Stealing Inmates'
IDs.* Gray Digital Media. July 10, 2014.
http://www.wctv.tv/home/headlines/Prison-Guard-Guilty-of-
Stealing-Inmates-IDs-266570751.html (accessed December 3, 2014).

"Teresa Giudice and Husband, of 'Real Housewives,' Are
Sentenced to Prison." *NYTimes.com.* October 2014,
2014.   http://www.nytimes.com/2014/10/03/nyregion/2-
stars-of-real-housewives-are-sentenced-to-prison.html?module=-
Search&mabReward=relbias%3Ar%2C%7B%222%22%3A%22R
I%3A12%22%7D&_r=0 (accessed October 19, 2014).

"'Winter Rain' Jailed in Fake ID Scheme." *The Bulletin.* The Associated Press. November 19, 2013. http://www.bendbulletin.com/csp/mediapool/sites/ BendBulletin/News/story.csp?cid=1374618&sid=497&fid=151 (accessed October 14, 2014).

The United States Department of Justice. *Los Angeles Physician Indicted in $33 Million Medicare Fraud Scheme.* Justice News, Washington D.C.: Office of Public Affairs, 2104.

Tighe, Kathleen S. *Semiannual Report to Congress, No. 66.* May, Office of the Inspector General, Washington, D.C.: U.S. Department of Education, 2013.

United States Government Accountability Office. *Driver's License Security: Federal Leadership Needed to Address Remaining Vulnerabilities.* GAO-12-893, Washington, D.C.: United States Government, 2012, 43.

Urban, Tim. "Why Generation Y Yuppies are Unhappy." *The Huffington Post.* HuffPost College. 15 2013, September. http://www.huffingtonpost.com/wait-but-why/generation-y-unhappy_b_3930620.html (accessed 18 2014, July).

Valencia, Milton J. "Cambridge man charged with stealing ID in benefits scam." *Boston Globe.* Aug. 27, 2012.

Vogler, Mark E. "RMV Document Theft Prompts Identity Fraud Concerns." *Gloucester Daily Times.* Gloucester, MA, April 6, 2012.

Zetter, Kim. "Hackers Finally Post Stolen Ashley Madison Data." *Wired,* Aug. 18, 2015

Author: Larry Benson
Director of Strategic Alliances – Government
LexisNexis Risk Solutions

Larry Benson is the Director of Strategic Alliances for LexisNexis Risk Solutions, and the creator of Fraud of the Day, a daily fraud publication for government employees, where he has built a following of 17,000 subscribers. Prior to his joining LexisNexis he has 25 years of sales and business development experience at various established and startup companies. He holds a BS degree in Physics from Albright College. An MS in Engineering from Lehigh University, and an MBA from Florida Institute of Technology.

Author: Andy Bucholz
Vice President of Market Planning – Government
LexisNexis Risk Solutions

Andy Bucholz is the Vice President of Market Planning for LexisNexis Risk Solutions, where he is responsible for strategy and product development for identity-based solutions within the Government Division. Prior to joining LexisNexis, he founded G2Tactics, Inc., a startup that built the first portable mobile license plate reader.

He is a recognized expert and frequent speaker in the field of data aggregation technology and he holds several patents in the field of data-gathering and mining technology. Bucholz holds a BS in Business Administration from The Citadel. He also authored the published book, *Police Equipment.*

Writer: Alana Benson

Alana Benson is a graduate from the University of Vermont and a freelance writer. She is an avid rock climber and teaches rock climbing.

Printed in the United States
By Bookmasters